UNWAVERING
VALOR

A POW'S ACCOUNT
OF THE BATAAN
DEATH MARCH

UNWAVERING
VALOR

A POW'S ACCOUNT
OF THE BATAAN
DEATH MARCH

FOREWORD BY ADMIRAL PAUL A. YOST JR.
FORMER COMMANDANT OF THE US COAST GUARD

WILLIAM T. GARNER

PLAIN SIGHT PUBLISHING
AN IMPRINT OF CEDAR FORT, INC.
SPRINGVILLE, UTAH

ISBN 13: 978-1-4621-1603-4

Published by Plain Sight Publishing, an imprint of Cedar Fort, Inc.
2373 W. 700 S., Springville, UT 84663
Distributed by Cedar Fort, Inc., www.cedarfort.com

   Library of Congress Control Number: 2014953618

Cover design by Angela D. Baxter and Shawnda T. Craig
Cover design © 2015 Lyle Mortimer
Edited and typeset by Deborah Spencer

Printed in the United States of America

10 9 8 7 6 5 4 3 2 1

Printed on acid-free paper

Clarence H. Bramley. *Bramley Collection.*

This account is factual—it did happen. It is the author's sincere hope that the readers of this narrative will feel a renewed sense of gratitude for their country and for those who have given so much in the cause of freedom.

Clarence H. Bramley never considered himself a hero, but in truth he was, just as were millions of other young Americans of his era. In remaining faithful to his family, his country, his fellow soldiers, and to God, Clarence was not unlike many others. Let us pray that succeeding generations learn from their sacrifices, and that those same qualities will continue to have place in the hearts of liberty-loving people everywhere.

May God continue to bless the
United States of America.

Contents

Foreword

The warriors that won World War II have largely passed on, and in a few years only we who are their children will be left to ensure that the story of their gift to us lives on. This is the story of one of those warriors: a man of almost inestimable courage, who endured torture and deprivation at the hands of the enemy beyond what most of us, even though hardened by service of our own, can imagine.

Clarence H. Bramley, a prisoner of war of the Japanese on the "Bataan Death March," was a member of the generation who saved the free world from subjugation. But more than that, he was one of the best. When you tuck your kids into bed tonight, say a prayer of gratitude for men like Clarence H. Bramley. Due to him and men like him, our world is far different today than it would have been without these heroes. Read his story and share in his pride and love of country. God Bless Clarence H. Bramley.

Admiral Paul A. Yost Jr.
Commandant, USCG (1986–1990)
Combat Veteran—Vietnam
Silver Star Recipient

Preface

Although as a young boy I was acquainted with Clarence H. Bramley and his family, I lost contact with him until only a few years ago. By then, my own military and other life experiences had enabled me to better understand the magnitude of his ordeal as a prisoner of war.

Clarence is a remarkable man. He has witnessed and been a victim of some of the most cruel and heinous behavior seen in modern times. Yet his objectivity and his faith have not diminished. Indeed, the opposite is true.

Curious concerning his life as a POW, I engaged Clarence in friendly conversation and was deeply moved by what he had to say. When I asked whether anyone had written a book about his experiences he said, "No, but maybe you will." While he probably did not intend that as a charge, I accepted it as such because of the importance of his story, and I am honored that he would allow me to relate it.

My father was a career marine and was a member of the First Marine Division in the Pacific Ocean theater throughout World War II. My friends and I were involved in food and gasoline rationing, victory gardens, and the collection of scrap materials for the war effort. Maps of ongoing military campaigns were posted on our elementary and junior high school walls. On display in many home windows were banners with blue or gold stars showing the number of persons in the household who were actively serving in the armed forces or who had died while doing so. Most of us had close friends and relatives who were participating in the war in

 some manner, whether on the home front or in military service. Although we were young, we were keenly aware of the war and its progress.

During the next major conflict, the Korean War, I became a marine fighter pilot and served with exceptional people, some of whom died in their country's service. As a lawyer and a judge, I have had close contact with dedicated public safety personnel whose lives are constantly at risk. Consequently, I have known many good men and women who have served their country valiantly and well. And I do not hesitate to say that Clarence is among the best.

The publisher's staff has been extremely helpful in the preparation of this book for publication, and I thank them for their expert and kind advice. When I was asked to identify the book's target audience, I replied that I felt it should appeal to everyone. I even briefly considered *What Every American Should Know* as a title. This book necessarily involves the Death March, but its primary purpose is to examine the conduct of the young Americans, and one in particular, who suffered the terrible experiences of the March and subsequent confinement. As the World War II generation ages and passes away, there is a danger that their sacrifices and bravery will be misunderstood or even forgotten. There are some Americans today who seem not to comprehend our flag's deep meaning and the freedom and way of life it represents. It is my hope that this book will help to enlighten those who are not familiar with the events recounted here, and to remind those who are. Even more, I hope that the life of this young soldier will inspire us all to be better human beings.

Herein is the record of a truly great man engaged in a noble cause.

William T. Garner
May 5, 2009

Since publication of this book's first edition, a number of readers have expressed to me their astonishment at learning of the events described in the book. One hopes that, having learned, they will not forget, for, as George Santayana famously observed, "Those who cannot remember the past are condemned to repeat it." Perhaps this account will motivate us to do what we can to see that there is no such repetition.

In addition, I hope that it will bring renewed appreciation for those who have sacrificed to keep us free. My late father, who retired after a long career with the US Marine Corps, once told me that public respect for members of our armed forces seems to increase in times of danger but decrease when danger is no longer apparent. I suggest that all sworn public safety and military personnel who honor their trust are entitled to our respect and support, no matter the season.

In this edition I have tried to broaden the historical narrative somewhat, but at its core the book is still about a man with profound faith in his family, his comrades, his country, and his God.

William T. Garner
December 15, 2014

Introduction

More than 60 million people died in World War II, making that conflict by far the deadliest in the world's recorded history. It was fought from 1939 to 1945 between the Allied powers (twenty-six nations, including the United States and the United Kingdom) and the Axis powers (a military alliance whose initial members were Germany, Italy, and Japan). The conflict eventually involved the armed forces of more than seventy nations and, as its name suggests, spanned most of the globe.

The millions of young Americans who wore the uniform of the United States of America during World War II earned the incalculable gratitude and respect of freedom-loving people around the world. Fighting with the Allies, they defeated the forces of tyranny and oppression. After struggling for economic survival during America's Great Depression of the 1930s, they went on to struggle for societal survival during wartime, meeting terrible foes with resourcefulness, bravery, and determination. We are left to marvel at their uncomplaining courage.

From the time of its entry into the war in 1941 until victory in 1945, the United States in reality fought two wars: one in Europe and Africa and the other in Asia and the Pacific. There is a view that at least early in the war, the European and African theaters received the greatest amount of attention from the administration, which led to the loss of the Philippine Islands (then an American commonwealth scheduled to become an independent republic in 1946). Whether that is so is left to the judgment of others. But what follows is the story of one young American soldier, Clarence H. "Clarie" Bramley, who was in the Philippines when the United States entered the war and who was among the estimated 12,000 American and 66,000 Filipino troops taken prisoner on the Bataan Peninsula. Approximately 10,000 of them died during the march that ensued and 25,000 more died during their subsequent imprisonment. Precise figures are unavailable—some estimates are even higher.

Clarence was one of those fortunate enough to survive the horrors and brutality of the Bataan Death March and the ensuing years of Japanese confinement. How he did it, what he contributed to his fellow prisoners, and how the experience affected him is remarkable. This is not a world or even a local history, only a personal one.

Chapter 1

The Early Years

L ooking for a job?"

Clarence stopped walking to survey the man in the Pontiac who had pulled to a stop beside him. Clarence was on his way to the bus stop after fruitlessly seeking work at the Procter and Gamble factory near Long Beach harbor. He did this every day, even though in 1935 a kid just out of high school stood a slim chance of being hired.

The man smiled, putting Clarence at ease.

"I sure am," Clarence replied.

"I'm the supervisor of a crew tearing down an old gambling ship. Do you want to work with us?"

"You bet," Clarence said.

"Then hop in."

Clarence did, and the motorist drove to a location on the nearby docks where men were dismantling a large ship, the *Rose Isle*. It had originally been used to transport passengers between Los Angeles and San Francisco and had later been converted into a floating casino.[1]

Clarence began work on the ship immediately and continued to work there six days a week, performing a wide range of assignments. One of his duties was to use an acetylene torch to cut steel into a few 18-inch squares to be shown to a Japanese naval officer. The officer came to the job site and inspected the squares. It turned out that the

Imperial Japanese Navy intended to purchase the scrap steel for use in the construction of its own vessels. (The irony of this was not then apparent.)

Clarence was the youngest person on the job, and at least a dozen other men were continually demanding his assistance. At first he tried to oblige them all. But he found some of their orders conflicting and, being unable to be in more than one place at a time, he became frustrated and decided something had to change.

Finally, he said to all coworkers within earshot, "Look, gentlemen, I know I'm the new kid around here, but I think I should have only one boss. When you can all agree on just who that is, I'll take orders from him. But until then, I'm not taking orders from anyone."

Clarence got his way when the crew supervisor, the motorist who had brought him to the location initially, told Clarence that from then on he would be Clarence's only boss. Clarence earned $4.00 to $5.00 per day, high wages for the time, but it all came to an end

Clarence Bramley and his parents, 1918. *Bramley Collection.*

when the tear down operation was completed in late 1936. It turned out to be the first of several short-lived jobs for him over the next few years.

Clarence Henry Bramley was born on September 25, 1917, in Salt Lake City, Utah, to parents who had immigrated to America from England. Clarence loved God, sports, his family and friends, flying (in spite of the fact that he had never flown), and playing the drums, though it was hard to say in what order. His hair and freckles were the color of a ripe pumpkin and he was at once exuberant and contemplative. Some called him mischievous. Indeed, his bishop[2] had once scolded him for crawling out of the church window during Sunday School class. But those who knew him well saw him as a dependable young man who was eager to face life on its terms, work hard, and honor God and his parents.

Clarence's family had moved to California in 1926, but he still had relatives in Salt Lake City. He was fond of that community and, being somewhat footloose and hoping for another job after completion of the tear-down operation, he traveled to Salt Lake City where he lived for a time with an uncle and his family. The pickings weren't what he had hoped for and he was only able to find work in a drugstore earning $1.00 per day. To make things worse, his only mode of transportation was a bicycle that he borrowed from his cousin. At a dollar a day, he couldn't afford to buy his own.

He hoped a better job would come along, but he realized that during the Depression he was fortunate to have any job at all. Using his uncle's telephone, he phoned his parents often and during one call was surprised and pleased when they told him, "Clarie, Mr. Blanton told us of a gas station job available for you here in Long Beach." Mr. Blanton had been Clarence's aviation instructor in high school and had not forgotten him, occasionally inquiring of Clarence's parents how their son was getting along. On the last such occasion, they told him they were anxious for Clarie to find a better job, maybe even one closer to home.

So Clarence returned to Long Beach and was hired at the gas station. He lubricated cars and earned the substantial wage of $4.00 per day. But that job, too, soon came to an end when the station owner decided there was not enough business to keep his newest employee working. Clarence then found work as a linoleum layer's helper for Lee's Linoleum, earning from $12.00 to $18.00 per week.

Once, when the regular linoleum layer was sick and unable to do a scheduled installation, his employer allowed Clarence to perform the job by himself. Mr. Lee was so pleased with the result that Clarence was thereafter considered a journeyman linoleum layer. His pay was increased, eventually reaching $25.00 per week. Clarence was then five feet ten inches tall and weighed 185 pounds. He began lifting weights to increase his strength and found that he enjoyed it.

ENDNOTES

1. During the 1930s, gambling ships, which were usually former ferries or steamships, were anchored three miles or more off the California coast to avoid being closed down by law enforcement authorities. Gamblers were ferried to the ships by water taxis from Long Beach, Santa Monica, and other coastal communities.

2. In Clarence's church, The Church of Jesus Christ of Latter-day Saints, a bishop is in charge of a local congregation and may be likened to a pastor.

Chapter 2

Into the Army

Knox Kendall and Clarence had been friends since elementary school. They lived only a block or so apart, and even though they attended different high schools, they remained close. The military draft was in force in January 1941 and both young men received letters from the draft board directing them to report for a physical examination. By coincidence, the examinations were scheduled for the same time.

After examining Clarence, the physician said to him, "Twenty-three years old and A1A. You're just what we need." Both Clarence and Knox were pronounced fit to be drafted.

Clarence turned to Knox as they left the medical building. "Knox, maybe this is the time. If we enlist now we can go into the Air Corps." Clarence knew that Knox preferred that to the infantry.

"I suppose so," Knox said. "Then we can stay together, for a while at least, and you can apply for flight training. I know that's what you want to do."

Replica of a US Army Air Corps recruiting poster, circa 1941.

7

Until recently there were only two ways Clarence knew of to become a pilot: one was to take private flying lessons and the other was to go to college for two years and then apply for military flight school. But the country was still in a depression and Clarence was trying to assist his parents as well as pay for his own personal needs. There was not enough money left for flying lessons or college. Only a few weeks earlier, however, he had learned that the Air Corps had a new program for enlisted men that would permit them to become aviation cadets without a college background. Of course, to become an enlisted man one must first enlist.

Clarence heard that the flight school test was tough, but he thought he could do it. After all, hadn't he attended Woodrow Wilson High School rather than a school closer to his Long Beach home because at Wilson he could take an aviation course? And hadn't he gone with Mr. Blanton to watch planes take off and land at the Long Beach airport? What did it matter that the class had only been a form of ground school and did not involve actual flying? Hadn't he done well in the class—so well, in fact, that Mr. Blanton had told him he would make a good flyer and even kept in touch with him after graduation? Sure, he could pass it. He could pass the examination and become an Air Corps pilot.

Together, Clarence and Knox went immediately to the main post office building in downtown Long Beach where they told the recruiting sergeant they were ready to enlist. They answered his questions and he filled out some papers. Clarence had heard that sergeants were loud and demanding, but he didn't find this sergeant to be that way. In fact, he was kind and almost fatherly.

"Okay, boys, just sign here."

"Does this mean we'll be in the Army Air Corps?" Clarence asked.

"Yeah, when do we start?" Knox asked excitedly.

"It means you're both on the way. You'll still have to take an enlistment oath. When we're through here, just go home and wait for instructions."

In both their cases, home meant the home of their parents. Clarence continued to work as a linoleum layer but informed Mr.

Lee that he would be leaving soon to enter the Air Corps. He only had to wait for the call. Most of the world was at war and both Clarence and Knox surmised that the Americans would soon be in it too.

In late January, Clarence came home from work and, as usual, asked his parents whether any mail or phone message had come from the Air Corps. But he received a different kind of news.

"Son," his father said, "we've just learned that Lennie is dead."

Clarence's thirteen-year-old brother Leonard had been riding his bicycle home from Orange County Park[1] when he was struck by an automobile. He was killed instantly. Clarence was dumbfounded. How could this happen to little Lennie?

Clarence's family was devastated and grief-stricken. Clarence was the eldest of three boys (himself, Herbert, and Leonard) and two girls (Lavern and Dorothy), and now the youngest was gone. After the funeral, he worried that his family might need him at home.

Bramley family in 1940, clockwise from left: Dorothy, Clarence, Herbert, Lavern, Bert, Leonard (center), Ellen. *Bramley Collection.*

"Dad, I haven't taken the oath yet," he said to his father. "Maybe under the circumstances I should ask the Air Corps to release me from my commitment. I'll probably be drafted anyway, but that might not be for some time."

"No, son," his father said, tears welling up in his eyes. "I don't think you could change it now if you tried. But even if you could, you must get on with your life. I think Lennie would be proud of your decision to serve your country. You know that Mother and I are immigrants. We came here from England before you were born, and we love this country. We chose it. And I can't think of a finer thing you could do for all of us and for Lennie."

Clarence and Knox soon received letters instructing them to proceed immediately to Fort MacArthur in San Pedro, about fifteen miles from their home, to be sworn in and to await further orders. Interestingly, Fort MacArthur was named after Army General Arthur MacArthur, who was the father of Army General Douglas MacArthur under whose command Clarence was to later serve. The young men remained at Fort MacArthur for about two weeks doing mostly kitchen police duty. They agreed that even though the work was tedious and not at all what they had expected, they would have a brighter future. On February 15, 1941, they were given the oath of enlistment and were ordered to Hamilton Field, California, for basic training.

Endnotes

1. Orange County Park, now known as Irvine Regional Park, was a public park in a rural area approximately 30 miles east of the Bramley home in North Long Beach.

Chapter 3

Hamilton Field

Located along the western shore of San Pablo Bay, and approximately 25 miles north of San Francisco, Hamilton Field had been named in honor of First Lieutenant Lloyd Andrew Hamilton, a US Army Air Corps air ace from Marin County who was killed in World War I. In 1941, the base was described by one observer as follows:

> An average of 250 clear days each year makes the mile-square, table-flat landing field ideal for huge Army bombers and fast pursuit planes. Field exercises and long-distance mass flights are the rule, rather than the exception, at Hamilton Field. . . .
>
> From the Bay shore, where a canal and wharf provided harbor facilities, the reservation rises gently to a velvet-green plateau on which the low Spanish-style structures of the post gleam white against semitropical plants and shrubs. Streets and boulevards wind about the hills. The administration buildings, hangars, hospital, theater, post office, shops and quarters, and radio, electric, and fire-fighting units form a compact self-sustaining military town.[1]

The morning of February 20, 1941, found Clarence sitting in the bed of an army truck with a dozen or so other young men. The sergeant escorting them looked back from his seat in the front of the truck and barked out orders: "All recruits get off here and check in inside that building, on the double!" Unlike the sergeant in the recruiting office, this one lived up to the loud and assertive popular image of his rank.

Clarence, Knox, and the other men jumped down from the truck bed. Clarence stood erect, momentarily forgetting his stiffness from the long ride. He watched the planes roaring and soaring overhead. "Wow, look at that, Knox. This is Hamilton Field. And those planes are the real thing. This is what we've been waiting for."

Main gate of Hamilton Field, circa 1941. *US Air Force.*

"Yeah," said Knox. "It all looks pretty good, but you heard the order. We'd better stop looking and get ourselves checked in."

It was hard for Clarence to believe that he was really there, at the beginning of what he was sure would be a great adventure.

That night he wrote a short letter to his parents:

Well, here we are at Hamilton Field. We arrived here this morning. We came by Pullman, ferry, electric car and truck. It's pretty nice here. I think I'm going to like it. I think Knox will too. Our barracks here is a huge hangar. There are about four or five hundred fellows bunked here.

Love to all,

Clarie

On March 1 he wrote two letters, one to his mother and grandmother, who were then in Salt Lake City visiting an ill uncle and other relatives, and the other to his father, who had remained in Long Beach. In the first letter he included this:

We started drilling (our recruit drill), Monday last. We are assigned to the 30th Pursuit Squadron for our recruit drill, which will last about six weeks. We have had about sixteen or eighteen lectures and have had what marching drills weather and inside space permits. When we have finished this drill we should be finished soldiers, we hope. In this drill there are a number of lectures, examinations, marching and hiking drills, pistol and rifle drills, as well as machine gun drills. There is quite a bit more than that, too. It's going to be quite interesting though after we really get rolling.

Thursday Knox and I were among a group from our squadron

assigned to K.P., or Kitchen Police duty. We were not bad though. It was just our turn. This morning we had our first official inspection. Our foot lockers, beds and personal appearance were in the spotlight. We did quite well, I believe. There were only four of our squadron assigned to K.P. for minor discrepancies. Knox and I were not among this number. We are keeping our fingers crossed though and are going to do our best to pass the rest. We have inspections every Saturday morning. Friday night this place really hums with everybody making ready for inspection. Next week I hope to start night school here at the field. They have classes every night in different subjects. I am going to take some Algebra and Trigonometry. We also have a physical examination once every month. The food here is okay. At this post we have plenty of everything and there is lots of milk.

As ever, your loving son and grandson,

Clarence XXXXOOOO

Clarence Bramley while at basic training at Hamilton Field, California, 1941. *Bramley Collection.*

The letter to his father was similar. On March 4 he wrote again to his parents with news of his activities at Hamilton Field. The uncle who had been ill had by then passed away and in addressing his passing, Clarence alluded to the earlier death of his youngest brother.

I am sure sorry about Uncle Joe. It seems to be coming in bunches. It seems odd, but I am sure the Lord has a reason. I want you to be sure and extend my deepest sympathy to Aunt Marie, Florence, and Wayne. We who have encountered this unpleasant experience can understand their feelings and truly sympathize with them. I would feel good if you have the extra money with you if you would use some of my money to buy flowers. I am going to write to Grandma. I hope she is taking it in stride. It is hard but you must keep chins up.

On March 11, 1941, Clarence wrote a letter to his father describing the continuing Army training and added the following:

We are nearing the end of our fourth week as soldiers and of being away from home. Boy it will be swell when our recruit drill is over so we can get home to see you all. We have a couple weeks after this one to go. Oh yes, last Saturday Knox and I got passes and went into San Francisco. We went to a show and saw "Gone with the Wind." It was a pretty good picture. Afterward, some of the fellows went to a dance but Knox and I walked down Market Street a ways and back and then came back to the field. I don't care much for Frisco. Everything's so packed in and the buildings look as if they were the ones built after the [1906] fire. It's too crowded to suit me.

Dad, I've thought quite a bit about Lennie, too. I bet he'd really get a thrill out of me being a soldier. The little tyke. Well, it's comforting to know he is always watching over us. It would really be hard if we didn't know he was in a higher place of glory. Try to think about that when his memory is stronger in your mind. His memory will always be in all of our minds. Sometimes it is stronger and comes more to the front though. It is then when we must think about the greater calling he is fulfilling. Thanks a lot for everything. God bless you and comfort you, Dad.

Your loving son,

Clarence

P.S. Knox says to say hello to you and all for him. Goodnight.

While at Hamilton Field, Clarence and Knox were billeted in a large aircraft hanger with some 150 other recruits from California, a similar number from Texas, and at least three other groups of like size from other states. They learned military skills and tactics. But this was before the United States entered World War II, and equipment was in short supply. Because there was a shortage of weapons, only 25 men at a time drilled with rifles while the others studied manuals. Eventually, however, all of the men became proficient in the firing, use, and field stripping of their rifles: the Springfield '03s (soon to be replaced by the M1 Garand) and .45-caliber pistols.

Each morning, the recruits assembled for roll call to hear any pertinent orders and to salute the flag before proceeding with the day's scheduled training activities. Clarence found that he was increasingly moved during the flag salute, perhaps because he was now wearing his country's uniform or because of the recent loss of his family members. Maybe for both reasons. After one such occasion, he spoke to Knox.

"Knox, I've been thinking lately about that flag. Have you ever done that? I mean, have you ever thought about what it means?"

Knox looked at the flag. "Yeah, I have. Growing up I knew it stood for freedom and all that. But I never really felt it as strongly as I do now."

"Me too. My parents were immigrants. I don't know how many times they've told me that out of all the countries in the world, they chose this one. I didn't have a choice, but they did and I'm sure glad they decided to come here. But when I think about all the people who died for that flag it kind of brings a lump to my throat."

"I know what you mean," Knox said.

"Who knows, we may have to fight for that flag someday."

Knox nodded his assent. Neither realized how close "someday" would be.

During a morning formation at the end of basic training, a sergeant assigned each man to a specific unit. "Any man who can type take two steps forward," he said. Knox was one of several men to take the two forward steps, and they were immediately assigned to a headquarters squadron at Hamilton.

That's great for Knox, Clarence thought, *but not for me. I want to fly.*

Before basic training ended, the men in Clarence's group were informed that if they wished to take the flight training examination, they would have an opportunity to sign up for it. Clarence and some of the others did so promptly. They were told that the physical examination would be in July and the written examination in October. Because he had requested the exams, Clarence was not transferred to another base after basic training. He remained at Hamilton where he was assigned to be a student at aircraft armament school.

During the days, Clarence attended armament school where he learned to arm Army Air Corps[2] pursuit (fighter) planes. In the evenings, on his own initiative, he attended classes on the base offered by nearby Marin Junior College to prepare himself for the cadet exams. The junior college classes were voluntary, but since this might be his only chance to take the exams, Clarence was going to do whatever he could to be ready.

After completing armament training, he remained at Hamilton where he was assigned to the 21st Pursuit Squadron, part of the 35th Pursuit Group. His commanding officer, First Lieutenant William Edward Dyess, told him that the squadron's prestige would be enhanced if he passed the flight training examinations while a squadron member. On August 4, 1941, he wrote his parents.

> *Well folks, I guess Knox has told you about me passing my final flying cadet physical. I took it July 28 and found out last Friday I had passed. I'm sure thankful I passed and I sure am going to try hard to pass the mental.*

For a young man looking for adventure, Hamilton Field was an exciting place. There were things to learn, friends to make, good food, an abundance of physical activity, a regular paycheck, and of course, the airplanes. *One day*, Clarence thought, *I might be flying these very planes.*

Among his new soldier friends were Bryce Lilly, who would later become his brother-in-law, and Kenneth Vick, who would become his best man. Bryce had been in the army for nearly two years, was about Clarence's size, had dark brown hair, and was a serious weight lifter. Clarence had seen pictures of Charles Atlas in body building ads and thought Bryce's powerful physique was more impressive. Shortly after they met, Clarence ran into Bryce in the base gym.

"Say, Bryce, do you mind if I lift weights with you?"

"Glad to have you join me."

"I haven't been lifting for very long and I never had any instruction. I thought you might give me a few tips."

"I'll try, but it doesn't look to me like you need much help," Bryce chuckled.

They lifted weights together throughout their stay at Hamilton Field and Clarence soon observed that even officers came to the gym to receive weight lifting and physical training advice from Bryce (who would often make excellent drawings to illustrate training methods and purposes).

One of many physical fitness drawings by Bryce Lilly, 1941. *Bramley Collection.*

Kenneth Vick was about six feet tall, well built, and had an accent that revealed his Texas origin. He was good-natured and had an easy and friendly manner.

On two occasions, Clarence's parents drove from their home in Long Beach to visit him and Knox at Hamilton Field. On one of those trips, they brought the young men's girlfriends along; that is, they were friends who were girls. Clarence had dated Joyce Hayes—literally the girl next door—for about two years, and while they were fond of each other, Clarence did not know whether their relationship would move beyond that. But he did like Joyce. He felt comfortable with her and they could talk easily. The girls stayed in a local motel with Mr. and Mrs. Bramley.

On Sundays, Clarence often attended church services in nearby

San Rafael. He was a member of The Church of Jesus Christ of Latter-day Saints (LDS) and religion was central to family life in his home. When he was a boy, his parents taught him to pray each night before getting into bed. It did not occur to him to deviate from that pattern in the Army. At first, he waited to pray until most of the other men were in bed, assuming that he would draw less attention. He considered the possibility that some of his fellow soldiers might be amused at seeing one of their number kneeling at his bedside praying. But if anyone had that inclination, or if they even noticed him, Clarence never learned. As far as he could tell he was not ridiculed, and he continued to pray quietly before retiring for the night. That remained a lifelong pattern.

Clarence had begun to wonder about something else. He had joined the Air Corps because he hoped to fly, and that hope might soon become a reality. But there was a general feeling expressed among most people he knew (and he had no reason to doubt it) that the war then being waged in other parts of the world was one in which the United States would soon become a direct participant. As a soldier, he would probably be required to fight and perhaps kill other men—or be killed himself. Vague thoughts would occasionally trouble him: *Considering what I have been taught and believe about love for one's fellow men, could I kill someone? Should I do that?* And in the back of his mind he pondered, *Will I have to give my life for my country?*

However, to muse in the abstract does not require commitment, and Clarence was so busy training that thoughts of dying and killing were submerged by more immediate ones, such as keeping up with daily military duties, preparing to pass the cadet examination, and communicating with family members at home. For the time being he did not dwell on the subject.

In his letter of September 5, 1941, Clarence informed his parents that he had recently received a fourth-class specialist rating, thereby increasing his monthly pay of $21.00 by another $15.00 for a total of $36.00 per month. He continued to share his earnings with his parents. However, in a later letter dated October 2, 1941, he informed them that a clerk had made an error so he hadn't yet received his fourth-class pay, but expected it the following month. He wrote: "I'll have a good pay check coming then. I'm enclosing a money order for $10.00 though."

ENDNOTES

1. Gordon Chappell, "Hamilton Air Force Base," accessed June 21, 2014, http://www.militarymuseum.org/HamiltonAFB.html (site discontinued).

2. On June 20, 1941, the United States Army Air Corps was renamed the United States Army Air Forces.

Clarence Bramley on leave at home before departing for the Philippines in 1941. *Bramley Collection*.

Chapter 4

Overseas

Clarence took the written aviation cadet examinations in early October but before receiving the results his squadron and group were ordered overseas to an undisclosed location. He was still a member of the 21st Pursuit Squadron. The men of the squadron only learned their destination while en route. On November 1, 1941, they sailed from San Francisco aboard the *USS President Coolidge*, a former luxury liner then being used as an Army transport. To the young soldiers, most of whom had never before been so far from home, the trip was both pleasant and exciting. While

The luxury liner *USS President Coolidge.* Launched in 1931 as a passanger ship, she became a troop transport in 1941. On October 26, 1942, she sank after striking underwater mines near Espiritu Santo, Vanuatu, where she remains today a favorite destination for recreational divers. *San Francisco Maritime National Historical Park.*

at sea, Clarence wrote his parents and grandmother:

The President Coolidge is quite a boat. In the days before it became a troop-ship, I imagine it was a swell liner. Of course it is still a nice boat, but I'll wager it was never so crowded with men in those days. There are several thousand men aboard, I imagine. We are quartered on the promenade deck and sleep in bunks that are four high and two wide and extend the entire length of said deck. I cannot say it is as nice as our regular bunks, but it isn't bad. They have similar bunks rigged up all over the ship. Many of the lounges and other rooms on the ship have been converted to sleeping quarters. We eat in the main dining salon. We have very good food on the boat. I believe it is quite a bit better than was expected by most of the fellows. There are facilities on board for recreation and other things, such as showers and such, and, outside of being a bit crowded, they are quite nice.

Our last glimpse of the good old United States for a while was somewhat dampened by rain and fog as both held sway Saturday the 1st when we left. The fog stayed with us for the first two days and it has rained off and on since we left. . . .

The last few nights we have stood on the after-bridge and watched the moon rise. It has been a full moon and makes a very eloquent scene coming up from behind the clouds and casting its beams on the water. In the daytime the water is a very pretty blue. I imagine such a cruise as this could be very nice under other circumstances. It isn't so bad though and is quite an experience for me, and I imagine many of the other fellows, too.

We do not know where our ultimate destination is. We hope to get passes to leave the ship tomorrow at Honolulu, although I don't know how long we are scheduled to stay there. . . .

I'm sure going to miss seeing my folks now and then. As long as it has to be though, I hope to make the best of it and to have something worthwhile to show for it when I do get to see you and be with you again. I know if I put my trust in the Lord and try to do the things I know to be right, I can't go wrong. If I live up to the teachings my folks have given me these should not be hard to do. . . . Write when you can and I'll write again as we go along and will mail it as soon as I can. Hoping this finds you all as well as it leaves me, and asking God to bless and keep you.

I remain,

Your Ever-Loving Son,

Clarie XXXXOOOO

P.S. Did you get the letter I wrote from Angel Island with the money order? I hope so. Excuse the writing please,

XXXOOO

In those days Honolulu was an exotic port, famous but not heavily visited. Hawaii was a US territory but not yet a state. On their arrival in Honolulu on Thursday, November 6, the soldiers were allowed to go ashore from 7:00 a.m. until 2:00 p.m. During that time, Clarence, Vick, and several other soldiers found a post office where they could mail their letters. They then had breakfast at a restaurant and later caught a bus to Waikiki, where they rented swimming trunks. They spent the next two hours swimming and body surfing. Tired but refreshed, they had malts and sandwiches at a nearby malt shop before sauntering through the beautiful Royal Hawaiian Hotel. After taking a bus back to Honolulu, they shopped, looked at the stores and people, drank fresh pineapple juice, and consumed more malts.

Several small groups of soldiers from Clarie's ship were also walking the sidewalks enjoying the sights. One of the soldiers called out to Clarie's group. "Hey, did you guys pay for that pineapple juice?"

"Well, we didn't swipe it, if that's what you mean."

"I only ask because around the corner it's free. I thought you might want to know."

Clarie's group investigated and discovered, too late, a nearby juice stand run by the Dole Pineapple Company where pineapple juice was being dispensed to tourists without charge.

On returning to their ship, the men watched natives diving for coins, a few (very few) of which Clarence and his friends had thrown into the water. At 4:30 p.m., their ship steamed out of the harbor as part of a three-ship convoy that included another Army transport, the *USS Grant*, and a Navy cruiser.

Clarie joined a group of men speculating about their likely destination.

"Maybe it'll be Tahiti," one man said.

"Nah, there'd be no reason for us to go there," said another.

"Well, maybe the Philippine Islands. I think we have airfields there."

"But how about Samoa or some of those other little islands? I think we have several airfields scattered around the Pacific."

Through the night the guessing continued. Early the next morning, Lieutenant Dyess finally informed them. "Men, I know you want to know where we're going. I couldn't tell you earlier, but now that we're back at sea I can. We've been ordered to the Philippine Islands. That's all I can tell you now, except that we'll be preparing the P-40s for active flight operations there."

Clarence knew little about the Philippines, but at least the speculation was over and they were finally going *somewhere*. He learned that the Philippine Islands were an American commonwealth over which the United States exercised authority over foreign affairs and national defense.[1] And as he considered the destination, he became increasingly pleased and anxious to arrive.

The *Grant* carried 23 fighter planes, P-40Es, the latest version of the Army Air Force's (AAF's) best pursuit aircraft. Manufactured by the Curtiss-Wright Corporation, the plane was called the "Warhawk," and it was said that with its 1,150 horsepower Allison engine, it could attain a top speed of 350 miles per hour and climb to an altitude of 30,000 feet.[2] That was exhilarating for a young man still planning to fly. Since Clarence was an armorer, he was also interested in the fact that this new "E" model was more heavily armed than its predecessor. Whereas the earlier "B" model had four .30-caliber machine guns (meaning that the inside diameter of the barrel was approximately 0.30 inches), the "E" had six .50-caliber machine guns, a significant increase in size and firepower.

After leaving Honolulu, the convoy maintained blackout conditions at night and arrived at the Port of Manila in the Philippines on November 20, 1941—Thanksgiving Day. Manila was located on the main island of Luzon and was the capital city of the Philippines. Clarence wrote his parents that day:

Well here we are, for a while anyway. We docked this morning about 9 a.m., disembarked, and were brought up to a field not far from the docks. We have been here about an hour now. We have been quartered in tents. No one knows how long we are here for. . . . Today is

Thanksgiving here. As a group there won't be any observance of it, but we sure have a lot to be thankful for. Things could be so much worse than they are.

Continuing the following day with the same letter, Clarence remarked:

We are fixed up pretty nice. We sleep on cots under a mosquito net. It's like sleeping in a cage. It's all right, though, as they say the mosquitoes are terrific. The net serves its purpose well. I enjoyed very much my first night's sleep here, which was also the first night on solid ground and in a pretty good bunk in a long time. . . . It sure is hot here.

Clarence set out to learn the Army command structure in the Far East, his new home. After a long and illustrious career in the US Army, General Douglas MacArthur, the Army's chief of staff, retired in 1935 and thereafter was appointed Field Marshal of the new Philippine Army, which he was helping to develop. In July 1941, because of growing ten-

General Douglas MacArthur and Brigadier General Richard K. Sutherland in automobile, 1941. *National Archives.*

sion between the United States and Japan, the US War Department recalled MacArthur to active US Army duty to command the newly designated United States Army Forces in the Far East (USAFFE), which included, in addition to all US Army forces in the region, the poorly equipped and not yet fully trained Philippine Army.[3] MacArthur's chief of staff with USAFFE was Brigadier General Richard K. Sutherland. The aviation component of USAFFE was designated the Far East Air Force (FEAF) and was commanded by the newly arrived Major General Lewis H. Brereton.

General Douglas MacArthur and Brigadier General Richard K. Sutherland at USAFFE headquarters in Malinta Tunnel, Corregidor, 1941. *National Archives.*

The FEAF maintained several airfields in the Manila area. Among them were Iba Field, 80 miles to the northwest, Clark Field, 50 miles to the northwest, and Nichols Field, 6 miles to the south. Because of the growing threat of war between the United States and the Japanese Empire, the FEAF was reinforcing its personnel and equipment at each field. Clarence's 21st Pursuit Squadron was assigned to Nichols, which was being used primarily for the coastal defense of Luzon and also as a control base for coordinating air, ground, and naval exercises.

Clark Field, Luzon, Philippines, 1939.
National Archives.

US Army planners were optimistic about the offensive potential of its new heavy bomber, the B-17 "Flying Fortress," being manufactured in the United States by Boeing. The first 35 of them were sent to the Philippines, nineteen to Clark Field and those remaining to Del Monte Field, some 500 miles further south, to be out of range of any Japanese aircraft on Formosa.

At Nichols, Captain Dyess (the squadron's commanding officer had just been promoted to that rank) notified his personnel that all pursuit aircraft were being placed on alert 24 hours each day, with pilots to be available on 30 minutes notice. All aircraft must be kept in flyable condition and fully fueled. Clarence and the other armorers were required to clean, calibrate, and test fire the .50-caliber aircraft guns daily, and keep them loaded. Cleaning was more time consuming than usual because the guns had been coated with a greasy substance called cosmoline (sometimes spelled "cosmolene") to protect them from corrosion and rust during the recently completed long sea voyage, and this had to be carefully and completely removed. Further, the squadron began intensive training in day and night enemy interception and air-to-air gunnery. All of this required that flight line personnel work from early morning until late into the night.

In the sweltering tropical sun, the ruddy complexioned Clarence often became sunburned, so much so that he acquired the new nickname, "Rosie," by which he was known for the remainder of his time in the Army. He tried to avoid direct sun exposure as much as possible.

In a letter from his parents, he learned that Joyce Hayes, the girl next door, had married someone else. He felt a twinge of sadness at the news but quickly became resigned to the fact. *I hope she made a good choice*, he thought.

ENDNOTES

1. With the 1898 US defeat of Spain to end the Spanish-American War, the Philippines became a US territory. Philippine revolutionaries, who had been fighting against Spain for independence, then continued to fight against the United States, finally surrendering in 1902 to end the Philippine-American War. The United States agreed to a plan for Philippine independence, calling for the Philippines to become a commonwealth in 1935 and an independent republic 10 years later.

2. "Curtiss P-40E Warhawk," *National Museum of the US Air Force*, accessed December 3, 2014, http://www.nationalmuseum.af.mil/factsheets/factsheet.asp?id=478.

3. On July 26, 1941, President Roosevelt recalled MacArthur, who had retired in 1935 as a general (4-star), to active duty in the US Army as a major general (2-star), and named him commander of USAFFE. MacArthur was promoted to lieutenant general (3-star) the following day and to general on December 20.

Chapter 5

War

On December 7, 1941 (December 6 in Hawaii) Clarence and the other armorers worked until 11:30 p.m. Three hours later, around 2:30 a.m., a Navy radioman in Manila received a message that the US Naval base at Pearl Harbor, Hawaii, had just been attacked without notice or warning by carrier-based aircraft of the Imperial Japanese Navy. That information was given to Admiral Thomas Hart, the commander of the US Navy's Asiatic Fleet, at his

Three battleships burn during the attack on Pearl Harbor. *US Navy.*

Manila headquarters. An Army soldier at Clark Field heard a com-mercial radio broadcast concerning the bombing and started the news on the way to Sutherland, who notified MacArthur.[1]

Several times that day, radar at Iba Field reported unidentified aircraft heading toward Manila or Corregidor. Each time, American fighters flew to meet them but were unable to make contact. Shortly after noon, while all of the B-17s and most of the fighters were on the ground, Japanese aircraft, whose takeoff from Formosa had been delayed for six hours by heavy fog, attacked the bomber base

Clark Field, Luzon, Philippines, after Japanese attack, December 8, 1941. *National Archives.*

at Clark and the fighter base at Iba. The first wave of 54 Japanese bombers struck Clark from 18,000 feet. Between bombing runs, Japanese fight-ers strafed the field. As Private First Class Victor Mapes of the 14th Bombardment Squadron stationed at Clark Field recalled,

About noon the B-17s came in to re-gas. They lined them up on the runway and the crews cut out for chow. I was listening in the barracks to a very loquacious radio commentator . . . when all of a sudden he said that Clark Field was being bombed. . . . Some of us went outside to the back of the barracks. Coming in over the mountains from the China Sea, up in the silvery clouds, were these two beautiful "V" formations of twenty-seven planes each. . . . We had our gas masks with us and were trying to get them on when the bombs began walking up the runway, like a big giant stepping down the line. . . . The fighters came in next and their machine guns were going through the air, cutting all around. . . . Everything was a holo-caust. It seemed like it went on forever.[2]

Aviation author-historian Michael Gough summarized the attack's results:

Fifty minutes after the first bombs fell on Clark, the Japanese flew back to Formosa, leaving Americans confronting death and wounds, destruction and damage, fire and smoke, and demoraliza-tion. When the Japanese flew away, half the B-17s and one-third

The Philippine Islands

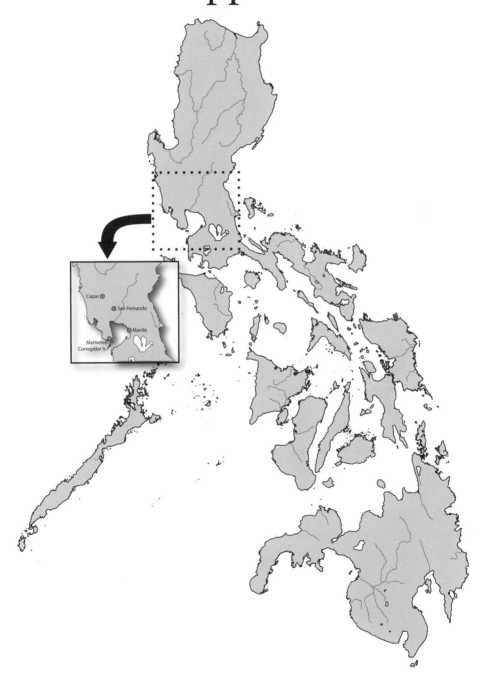

of the P-40s were destroyed, and two of the four P-40-equipped pursuit squadrons were eliminated as combat units. As surely as if all its planes had been destroyed, the fifth pursuit squadron, the 34th, equipped with P-35As, had also been eliminated from the war. Its pilots knew their planes were deathtraps in aerial combat with Japanese fighters.[3]

Thus, on the first day of the war the FEAF was largely eliminated—an enormous blow to the defenders.

On the second day of the war, December 9, at approximately 3:00 a.m., Nichols Field was attacked after its complement of fighter planes had left the area. The US ground forces at Nichols, the station personnel, were then ordered to other locations. The men in one ground unit were preparing to eat when the order came, and they had to depart without breakfast. Their cook told soldiers in Clarence's squadron to "help yourselves to the food," which they did with gusto. Until then they had eaten only field rations, and appreciated the better quality food prepared in the permanent station kitchen.

"What do we do now?" Clarence asked as they ate.

Nichols Field, Luzon, Philippines, after Japanese attack, December 9, 1941. *National Archives.*

"Sarge says to stay right here," one of his buddies answered.

Clarence remained at Nichols Field for two more days, sleeping under nearby brush and taking cover from bombing and strafing when further attacks came. He wasn't surprised when he was told that following the attack on Pearl Harbor, the United States had officially declared war against Japan, and that Germany had declared war against the United States. He and the other men of his unit were moved to Manila where they were issued .30-caliber Springfield '03 rifles and assigned to do night guard duty. They were housed in a Catholic school. They found that Manila was an attractive city with many palm trees and expanses of green lawns. However, each day they had to return to Nichols to service the few American aircraft that came in for minor repairs, fuel, and ammunition.

Over the next ten days or so, Clarence was told that Japanese ground troops had come ashore in northern Luzon and were being resisted by the American and Philippine soldiers there. These smaller landings were followed by a large and overwhelming Japanese assault at Lingayen Gulf on December 22, which the beach defenses were unable to stop.

The question Clarence had earlier considered in general terms—whether he could kill other men—now resurfaced. Given the present circumstances, one would have expected him to wrestle with the matter. But, perhaps surprisingly, it was not an issue for the answer was plain. He had taken an oath to fight for his country and he would do it without hesitation.

Clarence and other men from his squadron were sent to a newly constructed and camouflaged landing field to the north. It was so well camouflaged, in fact, that the first American pilots assigned to fly into it were unable to find it.

The few US aircraft remaining on Luzon Island used the camouflaged field and Clarence worked on the revetments being constructed there. These were mounds of earth designed to protect the aircraft and make them less obvious to an enemy. He also continued to arm the P-40s, including those flown by Captain Dyess and Lieutenant Sam Grashio, who both became well known for their bravery and flying accomplishments. The pilots were assigned to fly

P-40 fighter plane, circa 1941. *USAF Museum Photo Archives.*

reconnaissance missions only, but they always sought out enemy aircraft and shot many of them down.

Two enemy aircraft were shot down over the field and one of them appeared to be headed straight toward Clarence's revetment, crashing only 200 yards short of it. From the increasing air activity, the men accurately surmised that enemy ground troops were getting closer.

By weakening US air power in the Philippines and by delivering a near-fatal blow to US naval power at Pearl Harbor, the Japanese had effectively prevented the Philippine defenders from receiving reinforcements or supplies. It now appeared that the invaders would be able to come ashore in large numbers at many locations, as they had at Lingayen.

General Douglas MacArthur.
National Archives.

MacArthur correctly recognized the futility of keeping his forces in their scattered positions and decided to implement a contingency plan known as War Plan Orange that had been formulated years earlier. The plan called for his troops to be pulled back to Bataan to fight a delaying action from a more tenable location, all to allow more time for supply lines to reopen. MacArthur notified his commanders to defend only Bataan and Corregidor in the hope that relief from the United States would come within six months. The island of Corregidor was heavily fortified, and Bataan's mountains and jungles were considered defensible. Unfortunately, the stockpiling of supplies anticipated by the plan was still far from complete.

In an attempt to save the city and its inhabitants from needless destruction, on December 26, 1941, MacArthur declared Manila an "open city," meaning that all military units had been removed and the city would not be defended but was open for entry and occupation by the

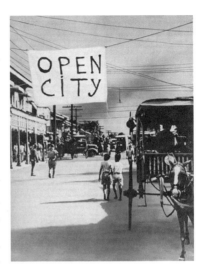

Manila, capital city of the Philippines, is declared an open city by General MacArthur, 1942. *National Archives.*

Japanese. Under the regulations of the 1907 Hague Convention, a city declared to be "open" was not to be bombed or subjected to artillery attack. In spite of the open city declaration and the pullout of troops, however, the Japanese began bombing Manila the following day.

On New Year's Eve, Clarence's unit was ordered to move into the beautiful but heavily mosquito-infested jungles of Bataan. They moved at night and became a beach defense unit on the

peninsula's western coast. There they were given two Universal Bren Gun Carriers, light tracked vehicles made by Ford Motor Company in Canada specifically for desert fighting.

"Whose idea was it to send Brens to the Philippines?" a soldier asked.

No one answered the question. It was commonly supposed among

An example of a Universal Carrier, commonly called a Bren Gun Carrier. *Photo Courtesy Hertmut Seidel www. AirVenture.de.*

them that the Army always had someone back in the states who sent men and equipment to various places without a clear idea why.

Clarence was optimistic. "Maybe we can use them. We can mount bigger guns."

Although the Bren was open on top, it was otherwise reminiscent of a small tank, complete with caterpillar treads. It carried machine guns of slightly less than .30-caliber size. The men increased the firepower by replacing them with .50-caliber aircraft machine guns.

The members of the 21st Pursuit Squadron were, for the time being, infantrymen, and Clarence was grateful for the training he had received that made him a soldier prior to learning to be an aircraft armorer. One of their tasks was to work with Philippine Army units to drive Japanese ground forces back from the area where they had recently landed at Agoloma Bay near Bataan's southwest tip. Beginning at daybreak on the first day, they pushed through the jungle some distance before encountering the enemy. When darkness came, they dug in and established a line. Although unable to see each other, they maintained contact by calling, "Contact on the left flank" or "Contact on the right flank." At about 1:00 a.m. they had to pull out because the Filipino troops on either side of their line had disappeared.

Because of the dense jungle and the inability of the men to see in the darkness, each held the ammunition belt of the man in front of him as they tried to return to their starting point. In spite of sniper activity, they were able to reach their destination. By then they were so tired that most of them lay down and fell asleep immediately—even though some were lying on cacti.

Working with units of the Philippine Army and Constabulary, the Americans continued in this manner for another week. The Filipino units were not particularly effective, or even reliable, but the Americans were soon relieved by the highly regarded Philippine Scouts, who had been trained by the US Army.[4] They were dependable troops and excellent fighters. After a few days had passed, Clarence's squadron returned to fight alongside the Scouts. The Philippine Army and Constabulary units had evidently been sent elsewhere.

In tough jungle fighting, the Americans and their Filipino allies

Philippine Scouts during bolo training. The bolo is a machete-like traditional Philippine weapon. *The American Historical Collection Rizal Library, Ateneo de Malina University.*

inflicted heavy casualties and drove the Japanese back to the sea. They then established a line at the top of a bluff. A large ravine opening onto the beach contained the dead bodies of a large number of Japanese soldiers (probably in excess of 600). In their retreat to the sea, the Japanese had apparently not had time to bury their dead, instead simply dumping the bodies into the ravine. If they intended to return later to bury them, there was no evidence of it.

The remaining Japanese troops were well protected in fully-stocked caves at the bottom of the 50- to 100-foot cliffs, and to force them out it was necessary to attack the caves from the sea. How the Japanese had managed to stock these caves, or how long they had been stocked with supplies, Clarence couldn't tell. The US Navy rigged some small boats with armor plate and cannons and used them to shell the caves. Men from Clarence's squadron, under the command of Captain Dyess, were also sent ashore to clear out the caves. Numerous Japanese soldiers were seen swimming away in the direction of the open sea, even though there were no rescue vessels in the area. The Americans shot and undoubtedly killed some of them and supposed that the rest would simply drown.

It was during this period that men of Clarence's squadron passed other Japanese soldiers who appeared to be lying dead on the surface or in foxholes. Initially, the Americans were surprised when some of the "dead" enemy soldiers rose up and fired rifles or threw hand grenades at the Americans' backs. Clarence and the others quickly learned that the Japanese soldiers were deceptive and if there was the slightest question whether a Japanese soldier on the ground was dead, they would have to ensure it by firing one or more rounds into him.

Three of Clarence's good friends were injured in this beach action. Maurice Freeland's wounds caused him to lose both legs just above the knees. Kenneth Vick was shot through both upper legs and the testicles, and the top of Bryce Lilly's head was creased by a bullet.

On yet another occasion, the Japanese anchored several large ships offshore and sent two or three smaller boats, each containing perhaps a dozen soldiers, to land on the beach. As the small boats approached, Clarence and the other American soldiers began firing on them, forcing the boats to turn around and set a course back toward the larger vessels.

"Look," said a soldier. "The Jap ships offshore are firing their guns at their own small boats."

"Yeah," said Clarence. "I guess they're reminding them to go the other way."

Japanese soldiers using a flamethrower on Bataan. *National Archives.*

"Well, they're not going to make it."

The American fire was accurate and none of the Japanese soldiers reached the beach.

But Japanese forces continued to land at various other locations along the coast, and for the next month Clarence and the men of his squadron engaged in pitched battles against them. While the Japanese sustained many casualties, there seemed to be no end to the number of new enemy landings, and the Americans hoped that reinforcements and supplies would arrive soon.

There were three airfields on the Bataan Peninsula—Bataan Field, Cabcaben Field and Mariveles Field—each housing three P-40 airplanes. Clarence's unit was ordered to return to aviation-related duty at Cabcaben, where crews were kept on the field around the clock. They bivouacked less than a mile from the field. By modifying the aircraft latch used for securing an extra fuel tank on the racks of the P-40s, Clarence and other armorers were able to load a 300- or a 500-pound bomb on each plane, making them more deadly in air raids.

By now, Nichols Field was in the hands of the Japanese. The P-40 pilots were still supposed to fly only reconnaissance missions, but they usually found action anyway and raided Nichols several times. The ranking FEAF officer, Brigadier General Harold H. "Pursuit" George,[5] together with Captain Dyess and the other officers, planned and executed a raid on Subic Bay, where many Japanese warships and transports had been sighted. Subic Bay was a large bay on the west coast of Luzon immediately north of Bataan, and appeared to have become a main landing area for Japanese troops and supplies.

One day, all nine P-40s armed first with 500-pound bombs and later with 300-pound bombs (in addition to their .50-caliber machine guns) spent the entire day flying numerous raiding missions on Subic Bay, returning to base only for more fuel, bombs, and ammunition. The pilots were so weary that after their final mission of the day, three planes ran off the end of the airstrip at Mariveles and another coming into Cabcaben landed with its guns still firing. It also ran off the end of the runway and into the trees.

A sergeant told Clarence of a meeting he had attended where MacArthur orally reprimanded his air chief, George, for allowing these missions. Later, according to the same sergeant, MacArthur heard a report on Radio Free Manila, a Japanese-controlled station in Manila, that Subic Bay had "just been raided by 300 American B-17 bombers flying from a secret base." The Americans had nothing close to that number of flyable aircraft of any sort and they had no secret base, but because of the destruction wrought by the nine P-40s, the enemy apparently assumed that the attackers had consisted of hundreds of much larger planes. As the damage reports came in, MacArthur told George that from then on he could run the Air Force his own way.

At Cabcaben, Clarence participated in the construction of revetments to protect the American B-17 bombers expected to land there. This was done by using a bulldozer to dig large holes in the earth a short distance from the runway. Each hole had to be larger than the aircraft it was to protect. The excavated earth was piled up around 270 degrees of the hole's circumference (similar to three sides of a square), making it reminiscent of a large horseshoe. The men then had the arduous task of using picks and shovels to complete the excavation and the building of the surrounding earth wall. At the open end of the horseshoe, the hole was extended out in a gradual upward slope to allow a plane to be wheeled in and out. Finally, from the abundant forest growth, bamboo and tree branches were strung between the tops of the earth walls as camouflage. The work was difficult, but no one complained because they all recognized the gravity of their situation and were anxious for the B-17s to arrive. Unfortunately, none did.

ENDNOTES

1. The Manila time zone is 18 hours ahead of the Hawaii time zone. The Pearl Harbor attack came on December 7 shortly before 8:00 a.m., which in Manila time was December 8 shortly before 2:00 a.m.

2. Victor Mapes, as quoted in Donald Knox, *Death March; The Survivors of Bataan* (New York: Harcourt Brace, 1981), 13.

3. Michael Gough, "Failure and Destruction, Clark Field, the Philippines, December 8, 1941," accessed Sept. 3, 2014, http://www.militaryhistoryonline. com/wwii/articles/failureanddestruction.aspx.

4. The Philippine Scouts, a unit of the US Army, was made up of Filipinos, usually under the command of American officers. Unlike the largely untrained Philippine Army soldiers, the Scouts were generally considered to be well-trained and to be a backbone of the American defense of the Philippine Islands.

5. With only a handful of fighter planes remaining, the FEAF was broken up as an organization and Major General Lewis H. Brereton was evacuated to Australia on December 24, 1941. Brigadier General Harold H. "Pursuit" George then became de facto commander of all remaining Army aviation units and personnel.

Bataan surrender, April 9, 1942.
National Archives.

Chapter 6

Surrender

Supplies of weapons, ammunition, food, and medicine were running low, but MacArthur had promised his weary and hungry troops that help was on the way. In mid-January, he ordered all unit commanders to give the following hopeful warning to their troops:

> Help is on the way from the U.S. Thousands of troops and hundreds of planes are being dispatched. The exact date of arrival of reinforcements is unknown, as they will have to fight their way through Japanese attempts against them. It is imperative that our troops hold until these reinforcements arrive. . . .
>
> No further retreat is possible. We have more troops in Bataan than the Japs have thrown against us. Our supplies are ample. A determined defense will defeat the enemy's attack. . . .
>
> It is a question now of courage and determination. Men who run away will surely be destroyed, but men who fight will save themselves and their country. . . .
>
> I call on every soldier in Bataan to fight in his assigned position, resisting every attack. This is the only road to salvation. If we fight we will win, if we retreat, we will be destroyed.[1]

As time passed, it became increasingly apparent to Clarence and his comrades that the additional men, aircraft, equipment, and supplies promised and desperately hoped for would not be coming. This was confirmed when General MacArthur and his family and staff, under orders from President Franklin D. Roosevelt, left the

Lt. Gen. Sir Arthur Percival, Gen. Douglas MacArthur, and Lt. Gen. Jonathan Wainwright. *US Army Archives.*

Philippines under cover of darkness on the night of March 12, 1942. They boarded four PT boats[2] and were taken from Corregidor to the Philippine island of Mindanao, flying from there to Australia. MacArthur's subordinate, Lieutenant General Jonathan Wainwright, who had headquarters on Corregidor, was left to command the remaining American and Philippine forces, while Major General Edward P. King, Jr. commanded the Allied forces on Bataan.

By this time, both Wainwright and King were aware that America's ability to send troops or supplies across the Pacific and to wage war in the Philippines had been seriously weakened. Whether it was for those reasons or because the conflict in Europe had been given priority over the fighting in the Philippines they couldn't say, but there could be little doubt that further help was unlikely. They were now on their own.

The Japanese were not the Americans' only enemy. There was also the jungle. There were great hordes of flies, mosquitoes, and other insects, and many of the men had already contracted malaria, dysentery, and various jungle diseases. To these were soon added scurvy and dengue fever.

Clarence suffered his first malaria attack in late March and was confined overnight to an Army field hospital where he received quinine. Medical supplies were nearly used up by then. The men were on less than half rations and were hungry and losing weight. They slept in hammocks they built themselves with the ubiquitous bamboo. One man, a corporal, observed a snake under the hammock of a sleeping sergeant.

"Hey Sarge, there's a snake under your bed."

"Oh? What kind?"

"Well, he looks like a python."

"How big is he?" asked the sergeant.

The soldier looked cautiously at the reptile. "He looks to be over ten feet long."

"Then let's eat him."

And they did.

Japanese Lieutenant General Masaharu Homma commanded all of the Japanese forces in the Philippines. The Americans and Filipinos, even in their weakened condition, offered far greater resistance than the Japanese had anticipated, slowing the Japanese advance in the Philippines so much that their planned offensive against the Dutch East Indies was being delayed. When the Japanese were forced to divert some of their troops away from the Philippines to fight elsewhere, the Philippine defenders were able to mount strong resistance against the remaining Japanese force. But soon

Lt. Gen. Masaharu Homma of the Imperial Japanese Army. *Public domain under Japanese intellectual property law.*

the Japanese returned with reinforcements and launched a major offensive against Bataan and Corregidor. Their troops were fresh, well supplied, and supported by a large number of aircraft.

The US Army Center of Military History describes the situation:

> With the attack stalled all along the line, on 8 February General Homma ordered a general withdrawal from the [Japanese] 14th Army's forward positions.
>
> Since 6 January the Japanese had suffered 7,000 battle casualties, with another 10,000 to 12,000 men dying of disease. The unexpected tenacity of the American opposition forced him to call on Imperial Headquarters for reinforcements. On the other side, the failure of the seemingly invincible Japanese to break through the defenses lifted American morale. Men in the ranks were anxious to pursue the wounded enemy, but MacArthur and his commanders would not permit such a counterattack. A temporary reversal of Japanese fortunes could not alter the dismal strategic situation. U.S. forces were isolated and could expect no relief in the form of men or supplies while the enemy could be reinforced at will. Any attempt to take the offensive would only consume scarce resources and exhaust the soldiers already weakened by the long period of reduced rations. The Americans and Filipinos directed their waning energy toward digging in and reorganizing for the next, inevitable attack.[3]

In fact, the American and Filipino condition did worsen. The long-promised help from home had not arrived, and with ammunition, food, and medicines nearly gone, and with no hope of replenishment, it became clear that the defense of Bataan, and indeed of the Philippines, was nearing an end. From this situation came a ditty that became well known among the troops:

> The Battling Bastards of Bataan
> No mama, no papa, no Uncle Sam,
> No aunts, no uncles, no cousins, no nieces,
> No pills, no planes, no artillery pieces,
> And nobody gives a damn![4]

Late one night, while Clarence and the other members of his squadron were in their bivouac area a mile or so from Cabcaben Field, they heard loud sounds of nearby artillery and were informed that the field had just been overrun by the Japanese. Clarence's unit immediately began to hike northwest over a mountain and away from the field, traveling in darkness. The next morning they arrived at a highway on the west side of the peninsula where they had earlier bivouacked. They were ordered to set up a last line of resistance there, but before they could do this a command car came up the road bringing word that the Allied forces "had been surrendered!" The men were ordered to stack their rifles.

Surrender? Clarence felt sick to his stomach. How could they be ordered to surrender when they could still fight? In his mind, and in the minds of most of his fellow soldiers, surrender had never been an option. On the other hand, what fighting could they do without ammunition? One of the men, who had run out of rifle bullets earlier, had simply thrown his empty weapon at the enemy. The few hand grenades they had were old and often failed to explode. Their food was nearly exhausted and many were sick. Clarence was told that 50,000 additional Japanese Imperial troops had come ashore that very day, fresh and fully supplied. Although the order to surrender was repugnant to him, Clarence was a young soldier trained to follow orders.

After learning some hard facts concerning their predicament, he

Maj. General Edward P. King, Jr. (left), surrenders American and Filipino forces on Bataan to Japanese. *National Archives.*

could understand the reasoning behind General King's decision. Had Clarence been in the general's place he might have done the same. Gradually, the other men began to express the same sentiment.

General King, who had had a brilliant Army career and whose courage was unquestioned, felt compelled to order the capitulation of his 78,000-man force, American and Filipino (the largest American force ever to surrender), because malnutrition and disease were accomplishing what the Japanese alone could not. The soldiers on Bataan had resisted far beyond any reasonable expectation, and to continue the fight would probably only ensure their slaughter. Without food, ammunition, or medical supplies, King assumed full responsibility for the surrender and informed his troops that they had not surrendered, but that he had surrendered them.

While himself a prisoner of the Japanese, King said to some of his men: "We were asked to lay down a bunt. We did just that. You have nothing to be ashamed of."[5]

Bataan fell to the Japanese on April 9, 1942. That evening the following announcement was made on the "Voice of Freedom,"

US newspapers report the fall of Bataan, April 9, 1942.
National Archives.

broadcasting from the Malinta Tunnel on Corregidor Island:

Bataan has fallen. The Philippine-American troops on this war-ravaged and bloodstained peninsula have laid down their arms. With heads bloody but unbowed, they have yielded to the superior force and numbers of the enemy.

The world will long remember the epic struggle that Filipino and American soldiers put up in the jungle vastness and along the rugged coast of Bataan. They have stood up uncomplaining under the constant and grueling fire of the enemy for more than three months. Besieged on land and blockaded by sea, cut off from all sources of help in the Philippines and in America, the intrepid fighters have done all that human endurance could bear.

For what sustained them through all these months of incessant battle was a force that was more than merely physical. It was the force of an unconquerable faith—something in the heart and soul that physical hardship and adversity could not destroy! It was the thought of native land and all that it holds most dear, the thought of

Japanese troops celebrate fall of Bataan, 1942. *National Archives.*

freedom and dignity and pride in these most priceless of all our human prerogatives.

The adversary, in the pride of his power and triumph, will credit our troops with nothing less than the courage and fortitude that his own troops have shown in battle. Our men have fought a brave and bitterly contested struggle. All the world will testify to the most superhuman endurance with which they stood up until the last in the face of overwhelming odds.

But the decision had to come. Men fighting under the banner of unshakable faith are made of something more than flesh, but they are not made of impervious steel. The flesh must yield at last, endurance melts away and the end of the battle must come.

Bataan has fallen, but the spirit that made it stand—a beacon to all the liberty-loving peoples of the world—cannot fall![6]

From Australia, General MacArthur paid tribute to his fighting forces. "The Bataan force went out as it would have wished, fighting to the end of its flickering forlorn hope. No army has done so much with so little, and nothing became it more than its last hour of trial and agony. To the weeping mothers of its dead, I can only say that the sacrifice and halo of Nazareth have descended

Surrender at Corregidor, 1942. *National Archives.*

upon their sons and that God will take them unto Himself."[7]

Captain Dyess later observed: "Though beaten, hungry and tired from the terrible last days of combat on Bataan, though further resistance was hopeless, our American soldiers and their Filipino comrades in arms would not have surrendered had they known the fate in store for them."[8]

ENDNOTES

1. Frank Steiger, "POW Diary of Captain George Steiger," copyright 1997, accessed Sept. 2, 2014, http://www.fsteiger.com/gsteipow.html. Clarence later recorded MacArthur's statement in his notebook.

2. PT (Patrol-Torpedo) boats were fast attack boats used by the US Navy to attack larger surface ships. ("PT boat," *Wikipedia*, last modified December 9, 2014, http://en.wikipedia.org/wiki/PT_boat.)

3. Jennifer L. Bailey, *Philippine Islands: the U.S. Army Campaigns of World War II*, essay for US Army Center of Military History, with introduction by M. P. W. Stone, Secretary of the Army, p. 19, accessed September 2, 2014, http://www.history.army.mil/html/books/072/72-3/CMH_Pub_72-3.pdf.

4. Frank Hewlett, United Press International, "The Battling Bastards of Bataan," accessed Sept. 2, 2014, http://www.proviso.k12.il.us/bataan%20web/BBBPoem.html.

5. Jay-Raymond N. Abad, "A King Among Men: The Story of a Forgotten General," August 2008, accessed Sept. 2, 2014, http://thephideltlegacy.com/articles/king/forgotten_general.

6. Colonel Carlos P. Romulo, *I Saw The Fall of the Philippines* (Garden City, New York: Doubleday, Doran & Company, 1943). Clarence also recorded this Voice of Freedom announcement in his notebook, but it was recorded sometime after his capture.

7. This quote appears in Clarence's notebook and was recorded sometime after his capture. It has been subsequently published in various forms. (cf. The Defenders of Bataan and Corregidor, New Mexico State University, and George Johnston, "MacArthur—A Great American Soldier Does A Great Job in Southwest Pacific," July 5, 1943, LIFE Magazine.)

8. Bureau of Naval Personnel Information Bulletin (March 1944). March 2002 Newsletter, *The Bataan Banner*.

Americans and Filipinos surrender at Malinta Tunnel Corregidor,
1942. *National Archives.*

Chapter 7

The March of Death

For four days, the men of Clarence's squadron remained where they had been when informed of the surrender. Then they were ordered to proceed to Mariveles on the southern tip of the Bataan Peninsula where they had their first encounter with their captors. They wondered what the surrender would mean to their cause and to themselves.

At Mariveles, Clarence saw an American officer and a Japanese officer shake hands.

"What's that all about?" Clarence asked another soldier.

"I heard they were classmates at the University of Southern California."

Clarence was heartened briefly by the exchange. But if the recognition of an old friendship between two present enemies seemed to herald good will on the part of the Japanese, Clarence quickly learned otherwise.

Although the Americans had given up their arms and were fully compliant with their captors' instructions, the Japanese soldiers immediately began to scream at their prisoners and to slap them and to strike and push them with their rifle butts. They searched the Americans and robbed them of their watches, rings, and whatever else they chose. If they discovered any item of Japanese origin, such as a photograph, money, or a military memento, the prisoner who possessed it was immediately beaten, bayoneted, or shot. Fortunately,

US and Filipino troops surrender to Japanese on Bataan, 1942.
Japanese soldiers loot Americans' personal possessions.
National Archives.

Clarence's few possessions were American-made.

Presumably, the Japanese had decided that any American who possessed a Japanese-made article had killed its original possessor and stolen the article from him. One prisoner was found to be in possession of a small shaving mirror carrying the words "Made in Japan." Such items were commonly purchased in the United States. The Japanese guard who found the mirror noisily lunged at him, slamming a rifle butt into his face. When the stunned and bleeding prisoner dropped to the ground, the guard continued to beat him in the same manner until he lost consciousness and his face was unrecognizable. His ultimate fate is unknown.

In the large pockets of Clarence's coveralls he carried a steel canteen and mess kit, two photographs (one of his parents and the other of his grandmother), a pocket-sized New Testament, and a larger book of scriptures that his parents had given him when he enlisted. He called the book his triple combination because it consisted of three books in one cover—the Book of Mormon, the Doctrine and

Covenants, and the Pearl of Great Price—all of which, together with the Bible, were sacred to him.

Some of the US forces had taken six Japanese prisoners during earlier fighting, and the prisoners were now turned over to the Japanese soldiers. The Americans were shocked to see their captors immediately shoot the six prisoners, apparently because they had surrendered or allowed themselves to be captured. There was no investigation or trial, not even an opportunity for explanation. There was only summary execution. The Japanese military had little use for any soldier who was taken prisoner, even if he was their own. What would this mean for the American and Filipino prisoners?

The Japanese then ordered all prisoners to form a line. Hundreds (and perhaps thousands) of Filipino civilians were nearby observing. It was apparent that the Japanese and the Filipinos disliked each other. While the prisoners stood in line with Japanese rifles trained on them, a group of the guards seized some of the nearby Filipino women and dragged them into the brush some twenty or thirty yards away. Clarence heard the women scream and cry and he knew they were being raped and beaten. But he was powerless to help. If

Prisoners hear orders from captors, 1942. *National Archives.*

only this were a nightmare and he could awaken!

The prisoners were divided into groups of about one hundred men with six to eight guards assigned to each group. Thus began the infamous forced march to San Fernando and Camp O'Donnell that has become known as the Bataan Death March, due to the thousands of men who perished along the way. As to each prisoner, the marching distance varied according to where along the route he had been when the march began. But for most, it was actually a series of marches covering approximately 85 miles, including a 55-mile march from Mariveles to San Fernando, 24 miles by

Prisoners prepare to march after surrender on Bataan, 1942.
National Archives.

railroad cargo cars to Capas, and another six- to seven-mile march to Camp O'Donnell.

The men were not told their destination or how far or how long they
were to march. They received little or
no food or water. Some were too ill
to march at all. Prisoners too weak
to continue frequently fell out of the
march. The stronger were usually not
permitted to help the weaker, although
many tried. Most of those who could
not keep up were bayoneted, shot, or
beheaded. Some were disemboweled
or thrown under the moving wheels of
Japanese trucks and equipment.

A Japanese soldier beheading a prisoner. *Source Unknown.*

The guards dictated the pace of
the march. Sometimes they would increase it by striking the prisoners with rifles or clubs. Their clubs had the appearance of small
baseball bats.

The weakened prisoners were subjected to a form of torture that
some have called the "sun treatment," from which those without
caps or helmets suffered the most. Many of the men were without headgear because they were either unable to retrieve their hats
or helmets before the march began, or the Japanese soldiers had
appropriated them. Even during the march, guards would sometimes remove the hat or helmet of a marcher. Each midday, while
the tropical sun was blazing, the prisoners were required to stand or
sit in direct sunlight for several hours. Their guards sat in the shade.

Even if a prisoner needed to relieve himself between ordered
stops, he had to keep moving. This meant, of course, that many
were required to urinate or defecate in their clothing, compounding
the difficulty of marching. There was no consideration for personal
hygiene.

The men were not permitted to have water, although often there
was fresh water close by and easily accessible. Many men went out of
their heads. The Japanese soldiers sometimes dragged out those who

The Bataan Death March, 1942. *National Archives.*

were delirious and buried them alive. Worse, they sometimes held rifles to the heads of other prisoners and forced them, under threat of death, to bury their delirious but fully conscious comrades.

Extreme thirst can drive one to seek water at any cost or hazard. While marching, some prisoners, nearly mad from thirst, broke ranks to try to drink from numerous clean streams or even from filthy and polluted carabao wallows. The latter were muddy puddles where the common Philippine water buffalo, known as carabao, sat during the heat of the day and wallowed, drank, and defecated. As with those unable to keep up during the march, most of the prisoners who broke ranks for water were shot, bayoneted, or clubbed to death. Those who succeeded in drinking the polluted water usually contracted dysentery, often leading to death.

A prisoner's life was entirely dependent on the whim of his guards. Some guards seemed reluctant to kill a prisoner, but most were brutal and appeared to take pleasure in it.

Clarence entertained thoughts of escape and even discussed it quietly with some of the other prisoners. He was told that some men had tried, and although most were killed, a few had made it. Even in their poor condition, it seemed to him that a hundred prisoners could overpower a handful of armed guards. Of course, they would have to consider where they would go and whom they could trust if they managed to break free. Clarence and other men who had been in the Philippines for only a few months were unfamiliar with the country except for the immediate areas in which they had served.

But there was a more immediate problem. As the prisoners marched, they were met by a seemingly endless convoy of Japanese trucks moving rapidly in the opposite direction. Most of the trucks carried newly arrived, heavily armed Japanese soldiers, many of whom were pointing at the prisoners and obviously ridiculing and insulting them. (The prisoners didn't need to understand Japanese to comprehend what the soldiers were saying.)

To his horror, Clarence saw some of the soldiers in the moving trucks swing their rifle butts into the defenseless marching prisoners, causing severe head and upper body injuries. He was later told by a fellow prisoner that other Japanese soldiers had done the same with rifle barrels and fixed bayonets, cutting and slitting the throats of an unknown number of men.

An unarmed prisoner might be able to get away from the guards, but not many could escape from such a caravan. Clarence decided that an escape attempt then would be foolhardy.

On the second or third day of the march, Clarence began to feel the cold chills of another malaria attack, more intense than the last. *Oh, no,* he thought. *Not now!*

Having been through it before, he knew what to expect. The chills would increase and he would begin to shake uncontrollably. After a few minutes the chills would give way to a high fever. His head would begin to throb and his muscles would refuse to respond to his instructions. He would then either pass out or simply be unable to walk, and either way he would then be killed by a guard. He began to shake violently and to sweat profusely. Then he felt a throbbing heat in his head and throughout his body. His thoughts were becoming confused. He must fight it. He must not allow himself to pass out. He must keep up with the other men. But how?

He felt one of his arms being lifted onto the shoulders of another prisoner. It was a soldier from his squadron, Aubrey Bissonnette, who

These resting American prisoners are said to have been required to march with their hands behind their backs. *National Archives.*

was quietly propping Clarence up. Bissonnette was what Clarence called an "old army soldier," meaning that he had served one or more enlistments in the regular army infantry before transferring to the Air Corps. He was older than Clarence and his bearing instinctively commanded respect. He and Clarence had not been close, but he was a welcome presence now.

Bissonnette spoke softly, "Rosie, don't say anything. Just lean on me."

He led Clarence, unnoticed by the Japanese guards, into the middle of another group of prisoners who had stopped and were sitting on the ground in what Clarence later recalled as a park-like area. Risking their own lives, some nearby Filipino civilians then gave Bissonnette and Clarence a handful of rice. Unfortunately, Clarence was too ill to eat it. Bissonnette led Clarence still further into the edge of the jungle where Clarence passed out. On awakening the next morning, Clarence was wearing Bissonnette's comparatively dry khaki uniform, which Bissonnette had exchanged for Clarence's own perspiration soaked coveralls.

Although Clarence had a full canteen of water when the march began, it was long since empty, and the marchers were still not allowed to stop for water, not even from the small streams through which they often walked. In some places the road was sand and gravel, but in most places it was just dirt. Thick clouds of dust created by countless marching feet and moving vehicles covered their bodies, choking them and making breathing difficult. Worse, it intensified their thirst. The tropical heat was beyond Clarence's prior experience and he continued to feel the weakness that comes from malaria, or perhaps just from being without food or water.

The word "march" had by this time become almost a misnomer. Certainly, it was misleading. It had never been characterized by the precision one might expect to see of military men. They were too sick and weak for that, and were becoming more so every hour. It was now simply a loose forward movement with some of the men barely able to put one foot in front of the other. Some couldn't and fell. It was now commonplace to see the bodies of dead prisoners alongside the road, many of them mutilated by bayonets. Clarence felt anger toward his captors but of a detached kind, almost as if he were only semiconscious. *Is this real?* He thought numbly. *When will it end?*

The next day, after marching three to four hours, the prisoners stopped and received their first food ration, approximately one-half cup of rice. When the march resumed, Clarence was still weak and feeling another malaria attack coming. A Japanese officer was walking with six or seven other prisoners, all of whom were wounded or noticeably ill. The officer saw Clarence and Bissonnette and ordered them to join his small group. Soon he had them all stop and sit next to a large group of prisoners who had apparently been sitting in an open area under the blistering sun for several hours. Clarence knew that the air temperature was well in excess of 100 degrees and he estimated the size of the larger group to be between 500 and 1,000 men. It was then that he became separated from Bissonnette, the man who had risked his own life to save him.

The smaller group of sick and wounded was then taken by truck to a railroad yard in San Fernando. There they were jammed with other prisoners into boxcars and transported by rail to the town of Capas. There was no room to sit in Clarence's boxcar, and even while standing the men were packed so tightly that breathing was difficult. Clarence was in a rear corner of the car. The heat was intense and the air foul and stifling.

In spite of their suffering, the prisoners did what they could to look out for each other. Because it appeared that Clarence was suffering a malaria attack, some of them helped him move to the front of the car near the closed door. There were small openings where fresh air could be felt. Although Clarence kept no count, many men died in the boxcars—but there was no room for them to fall.

From Capas, the men marched another six or seven miles to Camp O'Donnell. During that part of the march, Clarence had yet another malaria attack and passed out. Although he was unconscious, he later learned from other prisoners that a Japanese guard had started to bayonet him when another Japanese officer stopped the guard and ordered that Clarence be placed on a pony-drawn cart with five or six other sick or wounded men. Clarence's life was spared again.

It has been widely reported that General Homma was so humiliated by the resistance of the American and Philippine troops on Bataan (which had forced him to call for reinforcements from Japan) that he determined to take revenge on the Allied survivors. He told Major General King that the latter's troops would have to march from Bataan to their first place of imprisonment, Camp O'Donnell. General King informed Homma that his troops had been on short rations since January, were starving, and many were sick. In fact, before the surrender their rations had been steadily reduced from 4,000 to less than 1,000 (some reports say as few as 500) calories per day and 75 percent of the men had officially been reported unfit for duty.[1] King proposed that Homma allow the prisoners to be driven to Camp O'Donnell in the available American army trucks. Homma, who had been rebuked by Imperial General Headquarters in Tokyo and demoted from overall command in the Philippines, rejected King's request.

The precise number of American and Filipino troops who were on the Death March will probably never be known, and estimates vary. Some of the American and Filipino troops on the Bataan Peninsula at the time of the surrender died and some escaped before the March began. As noted, a few escaped during the March itself. Ray Hunt from Clarence's squadron was one of those. However, it is generally agreed that some 1,000 Americans and 9,000 Filipinos perished on the March. Of those who died, many had not been in a condition to undertake the March in the first place. Others were simply starved, beaten, and killed by their captors. But if any supposed that the dying would end when they arrived at Camp O'Donnell, they were sadly mistaken.

ENDNOTES

1. Jennifer L. Bailey, *Philippine Islands: the U.S. Army Campaigns of World War II*, "Philippine Islands: 7 December 1941–10 May 1942," essay for US Army Center of Military History, with introduction by M. P. W. Stone, Secretary of the Army, p. 19–20, accessed September 4, 2014, http://www.history.army.mil/html/books/072/72-3/CMH_Pub_72-3.pdf.

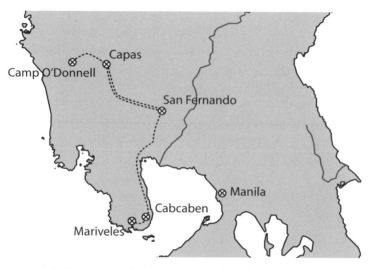

Map of the Bataan Death March. Single-dashed lines were travelled by foot.
Double-dashed lines were travelled by rail.

Chapter 8

CAMP O'DONNELL

Clarence found himself lying on the ground at Camp O'Donnell, listening as the Japanese camp commander berated the prisoners. The commander, a captain in the Imperial Japanese Army, seemed frenzied as he yelled at the prisoners in Japanese. A fat aide translated his words into English in detached monotone. Even without the translation, the commander's disgust and hysteria were apparent. He said that the rules of the Geneva Convention had no application because (1) the prisoners were not really prisoners of war but merely captives without any rights, and (2) the Geneva Convention rules[1] were not binding on Japan anyway. He insulted the prisoners and said that those who had died on the march before reaching the camp were the lucky ones. Clarence was too weak to be much affected by these remarks.

Camp O'Donnell was a partially completed former Philippine Army post, which the Japanese decided to use to house the men taken prisoner on Bataan; Filipino prisoners were kept apart from the others. It had wooden gun towers and was surrounded by a high barbed-wire fence. There were virtually no medical supplies in the camp, but one of the barracks was called a hospital and was designated for occupancy only by troops who appeared to be seriously ill.

Clarence was initially assigned to the hospital, but he saw at once that large numbers of the prisoners there were dying rapidly. Certain that he would not survive if he remained, he somehow managed to be assigned to one of several other buildings, each of which was about 25 feet wide and 100 feet long. There was a door on each end with an interior aisle between the doors that was about six feet wide. On either side of the aisle were bays—raised platforms— one of which stood about eighteen inches above the floor and the other raised four to five feet above that. These bays were sleeping and living areas.

While at Camp O'Donnell, the men heard that the American and Filipino forces on Corregidor under the command of General Wainwright had also surrendered. They didn't know how it could have been otherwise, but it was sad nonetheless. Soon, the men at O'Donnell were joined by men who had been the defenders of Corregidor, often referred to as the "Rock."

During all of Clarence's incarceration in the Philippines, the prisoners' only toilet facilities were open trenches, and work details were required to continually fill them and dig others. Clouds of flies darkened the airspace around the trenches and their sounds were maddening. Trench users slapped at the flies constantly.

At O'Donnell's main camp, where most of the prisoners were housed, there was little water. There was a single outside spigot for the prisoners' use and each man had to stand in line for hours every day to fill his canteen. Some died while standing.

Food was also scarce. Each man received a cup of rice cooked into a mush (*lugao*) for breakfast, a cup of rice at noon, and a half-cup of rice with a cup of soup for the evening meal. More often than not, the rice contained maggots and other insects. The soup usually consisted only of water and a few greens, but occasionally fish heads were added. There was no seasoning in any of these items, and the men had to expend valuable energy trying to keep the ever-present flies away from the small amount of food they were given. Dysentery from lack of safe drinking water and beriberi, pellagra, and scurvy from malnutrition were common.

While he was at O'Donnell, Clarence was required to dispose of the uniform he had received from Bissonnette and was issued a blue denim uniform, including a cap normally worn by Filipinos. Except for a subsequently issued G-string and a pair of shoes, this

Interior of prisoners' barracks at Camp O'Donnell, showing upper and
lower sleeping bays on both sides of aisle, circa 1942.
National Archives.

was to constitute his only clothing as long as he remained in the Philippines (although he somehow managed to acquire a pair of cotton gloves). He still had the canteen, mess kit, photos, and New Testament that had been in the large pockets of his Air Corps coveralls, but the triple combination was gone. Since Bissonnette had taken the coveralls, Clarence wondered if he had kept the book.

A burial detail at Camp O'Donnell, May 1942. *National Archives.*

Throughout Clarence's stay at O'Donnell, nearly fifty Americans and two hundred Filipinos died each day in the camp. The number was so large that there was a daily morning burial detail. The dead were carried in blankets held aloft by bamboo poles. Each body was carried outside the camp and allowed to slide out of its blanket into a mass bulldozed grave. After the grave had been covered, body parts were often exposed above the surface where early on they were eaten by dogs. But in time the number of dogs decreased because they were caught and eaten by the starving prisoners.

During their retreat to the Bataan Peninsula, the Americans and Filipinos had blown up a bridge north of Camp O'Donnell, and Clarence was one of those sent by his Japanese captors on a work detail to rebuild it. While on the detail, the men were housed in what appeared to have been an elementary school consisting of two or three buildings not far from where the bridge had been. Clarence worked on the cement mixing crew, shoveling sand and gravel.

All of his life he had enjoyed physical labor. Until food supplies ran low he hadn't worried about eating enough to remain strong. But now he was feeling increasingly weak and sick and he knew that he would only get worse without adequate nourishment. Beyond this, his fair complexion did not tolerate the tropical sun well. He tried to keep his face and hands covered as much as possible. Working on the cement crew seemed more demanding each day, and he made an effort to concentrate his thoughts elsewhere.

In spite of Clarence's cap and gloves, the sun's blistering effect on his face and hands was obvious. One of the prisoners said, "Rosie, your skin doesn't look so good. You'd better do something to get out of this sun."

"Well, that's no secret, but I'm like you. I can't just turn in my resignation."

Clarence suffered sunstroke and was carried by his comrades back to the school buildings. He knew that sunstroke occurs when one's body temperature increases beyond the ability of its internal cooling mechanism to control, and that it can be fatal. A guard tried to help by having other prisoners put wet towels on him. Clarence heard someone say that his temperature had reached 108 degrees. The same guard then had the prisoners take him to a pump in the schoolyard where cold water was pumped on him for several hours.

Clarence's fellow prisoners tried to help him remain out of the sun. The men were usually thoughtful of each other. But after a few days he had to return to work and sure enough, he suffered another case of sunstroke. He had to return to the school and noticed that his eyesight was beginning to fail.

Clarence later observed that his high fevers did carry a silver lining; he never had another malaria attack. He once commented, "I know that once you have malaria you're supposed to have it for life, but the only thing I can figure is that the fever must have burned the malaria out of me."

While Clarence was at the school, one of the prisoners escaped. He had been stationed in the Philippines for a few years and reportedly had a Filipino wife and children. Following the escape, all of the prisoners on the bridge detail were lined up and told by a guard that because of the escape ten of them would be shot. They would be advised later of the names of those to be executed. Work on the bridge stopped while the men anxiously waited.

After about a week, they were again lined up and were told by a Japanese sergeant, who Clarence thought must have been a veteran of many military campaigns, that because they had done good work rebuilding the bridge, he had convinced his superior officers that this time there should be no executions. This sergeant was unlike most of the other guards in that he did not seem to find pleasure in mistreating the prisoners. Clarence thought that under other circumstances, he could actually be a friend.

Almost immediately thereafter, the prisoners were told that in the future, without exception, in the event of an escape or escape attempt by any prisoner, not only that prisoner but ten others as well would be executed. The new wrinkle was this: in every camp, each prisoner was assigned a number and for any future escape or attempted escape, all prisoners whose numbers were within a range of five immediately above and below the number of the escapee or would-be escapee would be the ten to be shot. This system remained in effect throughout Clarence's confinement.

It is uncertain who devised this method of determining which men were to be executed—the Japanese or the American officers—but without the system, an American officer would probably have been ordered to select ten men for execution. In Clarence's view, the system that was developed was preferable. Because of it, the prisoners agreed among themselves that no prisoner would attempt to escape. They knew that to make such an attempt would bring certain death to at least ten other men. One of Clarence's friends in another camp had to watch as his own twin brother was executed in a similar circumstance.

Of the approximately 9,300 Americans and 48,000 Filipinos who survived the Death March and arrived at Camp O'Donnell in April 1942, about 2,200 Americans died by the end of May and an estimated 20,000 Filipinos died during the first four months.

ENDNOTES

1. As a result of controversial treatment of prisoners during World War I, in 1929 the International Committee of the Red Cross and various national governments held a conference in Geneva, Switzerland, where an agreement was drawn providing, among other things, that "prisoners of war" must be humanely treated and that the detaining power must respect their honor and provide for their maintenance. The Japanese government's official delegation to the conference signed the agreement but the Japanese government refused to ratify the signing. Nevertheless, it announced its intention to apply the Geneva Convention rules. Unfortunately, it did not. The Japanese point of view was simply that anyone who surrendered was a traitor worthy only of contempt and not entitled to humane treatment. To surrender was criminal behavior, to which suicide was preferable.

Chapter 9

CABANATUAN

After completion of the bridge project, Clarence's group was transferred to Cabanatuan Camp 1, the largest prison camp in central Luzon. Because of his deteriorating eyesight, Clarence was assigned to the hospital area. The word "hospital" was a misnomer, since there were no medical facilities in the camp. But there were some prisoners who were physicians and they were assigned there—although they had no equipment, medicine, or other supplies. There was not even water to cleanse the sick prisoners, many of whom suffered from dysentery. The hospital area was simply a cluster of two or three barracks where the prisoners who were too sick to work were housed.

The barracks for the entire prisoner population were surrounded by barbed-wire fences with gun towers at intervals around the perimeter. Some of the prisoners' barracks were occupied by field-grade officers while the others were occupied by enlisted men and

Prisoners' hut at Cabanatuan prison camp.
National Archives.

company-grade officers.[1] Barracks used by the Japanese officers, camp administration, and guards were located apart from the prisoners' barracks. Their area was also surrounded by a barbed wire fence.

While in the hospital area, Clarence was surprised when he was approached by his old friend, Bryce Lilly, whom he had not seen since the surrender.

"Rosie!" Bryce said. "What are you doing here? You're a sight for sore eyes."

"Bryce, is that you? I can't see very well, but I sure recognize your voice."

"Sure it's me." The two men embraced. "When did you get here?"

"Well, I just arrived. I was on a bridge detail and had a little sunstroke. I guess it affected my eyesight. How is the food here?"

"Ah, it's no better than at O'Donnell, if that means anything," Bryce said. "We just keep getting skinnier and weaker. But boy, it's sure great to see you."

"Maybe we'll be assigned to the same work details. It'll be like old times being with you, Bryce. Well, almost like old times."

Clarence and Bryce did see each other often in the camp and on details.

Clarence continued to pray daily. In his prayers he expressed his gratitude for his Savior, Jesus Christ, through whom all things would surely one day be made right. He asked that his family at home be protected, and he asked for the preservation of his beloved country. He asked for strength to face the following day, not only for himself but for Bryce and all of his fellow prisoners. He also asked that he might one day be permitted to return to his family. In spite of the wretched conditions, he had a firm belief that his prayers would be answered. Although he did not know the timetable, he did not have the slightest doubt that the Americans would return to the Philippines.

Clarence's eyesight became even worse. He had to move his small New Testament up and down to read it. Just as at O'Donnell, Cabanatuan had its morning burial detail and as it passed Clarence's view each day, he was able to see the upper and lower parts of the men assigned to the detail, but nothing in the middle. Finally, he became totally blind. He remained sightless for about three months, but thereafter an American doctor and fellow prisoner gained access to a small supply of canned milk, some of which he gave to Clarence, and his sight returned. He was then able to return to regular duty.

During Clarence's period of complete blindness, he was leaning against a hospital barracks building one day when he was spotted by Aubrey Bissonnette. They had not had contact with each other since the Death March. Their excited greetings were followed by a lengthy conversation, during which Clarence said, "I've been wanting to thank you. You know, if you hadn't helped me on the March, I'd probably be dead."

Clarence could hear the smile in Bissonnette's voice as he said, "Oh, you'd have done the same for me."

Clarence wondered if he was saying too much or not enough, but what do you tell a man who has saved your life? You can never forget him and you can never fully express your appreciation. Their talk turned to other things.

Clarence remembered his triple combination. "By the way, when you changed clothes with me, did you notice whether there was a book of scriptures in my coveralls?"

"Oh, yes, I remember it. At first I thought I had taken everything out of your pockets and put them in the clothes I gave you. Later, I saw that I had missed that book, but by then you were gone. To be honest, I didn't think I would ever see you again so I gave the book to a guy from Oregon. I heard later that he died."

Clarence hoped that the soldier from Oregon was able to read the book and gain some comfort from it before he passed away.

Although some Japanese officers and a few guards showed a degree of kindness to the prisoners, most did not. They seemed to share the view that their Caucasian prisoners, having surrendered, were to be despised and treated without mercy. The Japanese were physically smaller than the Americans, although many were quite strong, and Clarence thought they might be suffering from a "little-man" complex and needed to strut and bully to stroke their own ego and demonstrate their supposed superiority.

The guards often reminded the Americans that they were "lower than dogs." Clarence could see that the Japanese antipathy toward their Filipino prisoners was even stronger. He surmised that this was because the Filipinos had once surrendered to the Americans, an act that was unconscionable to the Japanese; on top of that, they had later agreed that the Philippines could become an American commonwealth—subject to extensive control by the United States.

Often when guards determined that a prisoner was being belligerent, they would tie the prisoner's wrists together with one end of a rope and wrap the other end around an overhead beam or fence, leaving the prisoner suspended in the air for hours or even days with only his toes making contact with the ground. Many prisoners died from this treatment while others suffered permanent physical injury.

Beatings were routinely administered, sometimes for not following the rules and sometimes for no reason at all. Prisoners were executed on the same basis. Their bodies were then tied to buildings or fences in plain view. Clarence saw a guard swaggering while holding aloft on his bayoneted rifle the severed head of a prisoner. All of this served as a reminder that the Japanese were in total control.

How can men treat other men so? Clarence thought angrily. Although he was not ordinarily a violent man, it took enormous effort to resist the impulse to seek vengeance on his captors. Resentment among the prisoners was strong, but to express it was useless and would likely result in death. Nevertheless, it was not uncommon for a prisoner to smile while cursing his non-English-understanding guard.

The work details sometimes entailed leaving the main camp for many weeks, and the Americans tried to assign a physician and a chaplain to each lengthy detail. However, the Japanese officers routinely and systematically removed them. Clarence decided that this was for the purpose of lowering prisoner morale. To counter the effect of the removals, the imprisoned officers preparing the roster tried to include men with medical experience, such as a medic or another soldier with advanced first aid training; and men with church experience, such as a chaplain's assistant or simply an active churchgoer.

In the main camp, the chaplains conducted Protestant and

Catholic worship services each Sunday, even though the services were sometimes only lightly attended. Clarence always tried to attend one of these, but there could be no such services for the men away on work details. The chief chaplain, A.C. Oliver, Jr., told the prisoners during a Sunday service that it would be up to the men themselves to conduct their own services when they were away from the main camp. Clarence and another prisoner, Jesse Miller, began to do this. Although Clarence met only one other member of his church while a prisoner of war, a handful of other prisoners attended the services he conducted. The LDS soldier was Franklin East from Pomerene, Arizona, and to Clarence's delight, he gave Clarence a copy of the Book of Mormon.

The prisoners did not have any formal observance of major holidays, such as Christmas, Easter, or the 4th of July. If they were in the main camp on or near those times, they were able to hear references to them in the regular Sunday services. Otherwise, the men would simply remind each other of the occasion and express their best wishes.

One might suppose that the talk among the prisoners was mostly about women. In reality, the major topics were food, freedom, and families. Sometimes other prisoners would ask Clarence in substance, "Rosie, do you think we'll ever have enough food?" "Do you think this war will ever end?" "Do you think we'll ever make it home?" Clarence was unsure why these questions were so often directed to him. Perhaps because he prayed often the questioners thought his words might be prophetic. Then again, perhaps the questions were only rhetorical and answers were not really expected. But Clarence's responses were always the same.

"Sure, it'll be over one of these days. We're Americans! Our boys will be back in the Philippines and we'll be freed, and then we'll be able to eat whatever we want. All we have to do is make it through one day at a time and before you know it, we'll be home."

The prisoners' food was prepared in the camp kitchen by assigned fellow prisoners. The menu was always rice, and not much of it. Try as they might to find different ways to cook it, it was still rice. Some guards would beat any prisoner who picked edible weeds to add to the rice or soup, but other guards would not. The men soon learned who was in each category. Sometimes a man would catch a rat or a lizard or a snake and it would be added to the rice for variety. Prisoners who were too sick to work were given even less food than those who could. The Japanese said that a sick man did not need as much food as a well man. Consequently, the sick usually got worse.

Clarence managed to obtain a job in the kitchen. It was physically demanding work because the iron pots in which the rice was cooked were three feet in diameter and heavy, and he had to lift them continually. But at the same time he felt fortunate to have the assignment because in the kitchen he was not exposed to the sun and, of at least equal importance, he was able to eat the rice residue that he scraped from the pots after the prisoners' meals. The American cavalry officer in charge of the kitchen, Major Chandler, was impressed with Clarence's work habits and was able to have him assigned as an orderly in a *bahay*, living quarters Chandler shared with seven other field-grade officers. While he was there, however, Clarence was often sent to work on the prison farm.

The prisoners were almost routinely slapped in the face by their guards. Once, a Japanese officer instructed Clarence to proceed to a location used to store the officers' food and bring him a barrel of squid. Clarence did so, but he was unaware that other prisoners had found the barrel earlier and had removed some of its contents. When the officer discovered that squid had already been taken from the barrel, he struck Clarence across the face with his swagger stick. However, when he learned later that Clarence had not taken the food, he apologized. Clarence knew by now that while most of his captors were brutal, some were humane. The trick was to know the difference.

Survival required a sense of humor. On the prison farm, Clarence was part of a crew of prisoners planting rice in the rice paddies. This required them to bend low to place the rice shoots in ankle deep water and mud. He worked alongside a tall, lanky

Texan. For some reason (or for none at all), a Japanese guard kicked the Texan in the back, sending him sprawling into the paddy. When the prisoner raised his muddy body erect, he loudly drawled, "You really shouldn't complain at these wages."

One of the Cabanatuan guards was known by the prisoners as Donald Duck and they often called him by that name. After a few days he seemed to suspect that his new title was not flattering. He asked, "Who is Donald Duck?"

One prisoner said, "Oh, he's a famous movie star."

The guard appeared satisfied with that answer, but only temporarily. Somehow he learned Donald's true identity and he angrily pointed his rifle at one of the prisoners as if preparing to shoot. Thereafter, the prisoners discontinued using the name in the guard's presence and they tried to avoid him as much as possible.

Clarence learned enough of the Japanese language to understand most of the orders given by the guards. (For example, he learned quickly that *kuda* meant "get going.") One work detail required the prisoners to perform a simulated surrender to Japanese forces in front of cameramen filming a Japanese motion picture. Although distasteful to Clarence and the other prisoners, they marched and lifted their arms on cue as ordered by their guards.

Until April 14, 1943, Clarence's parents knew only that he was "missing in action." On that date they received the following telegram from the Army adjutant general:

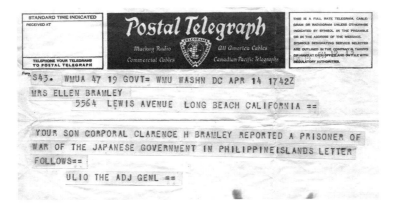

The letter that followed explained that they could communicate with Clarence by way of official prisoner-of-war mail. This was usually in the form of postcards, limited to 50 words, and it took about a year for delivery. All mail was censored and Clarence was able to say only that he was well and hoped they were too. Nevertheless, they were able to exchange two to three cards and one equally brief single page letter in this manner during the time Clarence remained in the Philippines.

POW mail, always censored by Japanese military. *Bramley Collection.*

Bryce Lilly was assigned to a work detail being sent to another prison camp run by Japanese Marines, and Clarence volunteered for the same detail knowing that if he wasn't there, he would be assigned to another detail anyway. By volunteering he could spend more time with his friend. On this assignment, which was known as the Las Pinas project, the prisoners, weak and emaciated from sickness and hunger, were ordered to build an airfield. Clarence knew that the prisoners' only value to their captors was as slave labor and that to continue living one must continue working, so he worked.

First, the men drained rice paddies by digging through the earthen dikes and allowing the water to run off. Then they leveled the terrain by moving earth from hilly areas to low ones. They did this by using picks and shovels and by hand-loading and manually pushing small railcars of dirt on narrow gauge tracks. As each hill was leveled, they lifted the track and moved it to the next hill. Using the same system, they brought rocks from a creek bed about a quarter mile away and placed them in the earth where the landing strip was to be located. They then raked the dirt and planted sod that the Japanese had removed from areas around the city of Manila. Atop this they placed steel mats taken by the Japanese from American supplies.

The landing strip was used to train new pilots, and Clarence once saw a light transport plane run off the end of the steel mats and sink a foot or so into the earth. It rained often and after one rainstorm, a bulldozer that had been parked on a filled area sank out of sight.

The work at the airfield was arduous and exhausting and there was little time for rest. The prisoners were supervised by a group of very young Japanese boys who appeared to be between the ages of 10 and 12. These boys had clubs (perhaps pick handles) with which they beat prisoners who they felt were moving too slowly. The boys were backed up by guards with rifles. If a prisoner talked back to one of the boys, a guard struck the prisoner with his rifle butt. One American prisoner was so weary and fatigued that when a

Foreground: Newspaper clippings from the Bramley Collection. Background: Japanese Army "Ann" bombers over the main line on Bataan courtesy of the US Air Force.

Corporal Held in Jap Prison

Clarence H. Brumley, son of Mr. and Mrs. Herbert Brumley, 5564 Lewis Avenue, is now a prisoner of war in the Philippine Islands.

Corporal Brumley, 25, was born in Salt Lake City, Utah, and lived here for 16 years, attending Jane Addams elementary, Lindbergh Junior High and Wilson High Schools, graduating from the latter in 1935.

Prior to his entrance into the Army Air Corps in March, 1940, he was employed by a linoleum firm. The family received a card from him not long ago while in the prison camp, saying that he was well, and to send his best regards to all his friends.

Soldier Reported Prisoner of Japs

april 13, 43

Corporal Clarence H. Bramley of 5564 Lewis Avenue, who was reported missing in the Battle of Bataan, is a prisoner of war in the Philippine Islands, according to information sent by the War Department to his parents, Mr. and Mrs. Herbert Bramley.

No Word Received From Corporal for Over Year

No word of Cpl. Clarence H. Bramley, 27, has been received by his parents, Mr. and Mrs. Herbert Bramley of 5564 Lewis Ave., for more than a year. He went overseas with the 21st Pursuit Squadron in October, 1941, and was reported missing in August, 1942. Later it was learned he had been taken prisoner on Bataan.

Two cards written by Cpl. Bramley in January, 1944, while in Camp No. 4 on the Philippines reached his parents a year later. Several of his comrades at the prison who have been returned to this country have been unable to give any recent information of him.

A brother, 2nd Lieut. Herbert G. Bramley, recently spent a 10-day furlough here after receiving his commission April 15 at Turner Field, Albay, Ga., accompanied by his wife, the former Wanda Setton of Long Beach. The officer has gone to Madison, Wis., for new assignment.

North Long Beach Boy Reported As Missing, Found In Jap Prison

— BUY STAMPS —

—BUY BONDS—

Mr. and Mrs. Herbert Bromley, of 5564 Lewis avenue, are just about the happiest couple in North Long Beach these days. Wednesday afternoon they received a message from the war department that their son, Clarence, is a prisoner in the Philippines, having been captured by the Japs. They had received word last August that their son was missing in action since May 7th and nothing had been heard since until the message on Wednesday.

april 14th 1943
L.B. Argus

guard began to strike him in the back with a rifle, he placed his arm behind his back in a defensive posture as if to absorb the blow. His actual purpose was to suffer a wounded arm so he could rest. His arm was fractured and he did get a few days off.

Clarence noted that most of the boy-supervisors were timid when they began their service, reluctant to strike a hard blow on a prisoner. But with the encouragement of the guards, they soon began to swing their clubs with authority. Even though there were many Japanese soldiers who were only boys in their early teens, it appeared that these supervisors were even younger, not yet able to be soldiers. At night they were sometimes heard in their barracks crying for their mothers.

A prisoner never knew for certain what work detail he would be assigned to until the project actually started. Because there were many jobs, some lasting days and others weeks, Clarence eventually became acquainted with most of the prisoners in the camp. On the Las Pinas project he met John Cotten, a young soldier from Bartlesville, Oklahoma. John was slightly younger than Clarence, about the same height, friendly, and good-natured. Under normal circumstances, John might have been more slender than Clarence, but by this time everyone was thin in the extreme so it was hard to tell. They talked together about what most of the others talked about: food, families, and their hope that the Americans would soon win the war. Clarence enjoyed John's company.

While working on the Las Pinas project, Clarence and other

Red Cross Aid Sought to Get Note Through

Notified by the War Department that her son, Corporal Clarence H. Bramley, listed as missing since May, is a prisoner in the Philippines, Mrs. Herbert Bramley, 5564 Lewis Avenue, is seeking to correspond with him through the International Red Cross.

Corporal Bramley, 25, went to the Philippines with the Army Air Forces in November, 1941, and shortly before Pearl Harbor was appointed an aviation cadet.

CORP. BRAMLEY.

From him Mr. and Mrs. Bramley received a Christmas radiogram saying he was at Nichols Field and "all well." In a letter mailed in February from Bataan, Bramley reported that the "men are in good spirits." How the letter, the only one she received from her son after the outbreak of the war, was brought from Bataan Mrs. Bramley does not know.

Solidarity of the Philippine people with American troops was described by Bramley in the letter. "The natives are very friendly. From babes in arms to the oldest persons there is one thing they all know and understand: The 'V' for victory. Whenever any of our troops go by the natives will all hold up their two forefingers in a 'V' and holler, 'Victory.'"

prisoners were housed in a building that had formerly been a school-house. Inside the building, Clarence had the good fortune to find an unused notebook. He had a pencil, so he began to use the notebook to record whatever he felt would help him while conducting religious services when a chaplain was unavailable. He also recorded quotes and ideas he found inspiring or helpful, and some names and hometown addresses of fellow prisoners (including officers for whom he had worked as an orderly).

He even recorded poetry. Some of the prisoners wrote poetry to give expression to their sentiments, lift their spirits, or try to make sense of their condition. Clarence included some of their poetry in the notebook.[2]

About twice a year, at irregular intervals, Clarence and the other prisoners received special treats in the form of Red Cross packages. These were mostly from the American Red Cross, but some came from the Canadian and French Red Cross organizations and some even came from a church in Manila. Generally, each package was marked for sharing by two or three men. The Red Cross packages usually contained cigarettes. Since paper was generally unavailable to the prisoners, they would use the back of the cigarette packages for writing material. Although Clarence did not smoke, he was able to retrieve empty cigarette packages from other prisoners. He recorded information on the back of the packs and later bound[3] them into a journal. In this manner, he recorded the contents of the Red Cross packages they received. As an example, on November 24, 1943, he recorded receiving a package containing the following:

1 can Klim powdered milk	2 type-B chocolate bars
2 cans Spam	2 bars Swan soap
1 can grape jam	½ lb. Kraft American Cheese
½ pound box Sugar Dots	1 can liver pate
2 cans soluble coffee	2 pkgs. cigarettes
1 can opener	3 cans corned beef
4 cans Kraft preserved butter	1 box prunes
	1 can salmon

On another occasion he recorded having received these nonfood items:

1 razor and 6 blades	1 pencil
1 shaving cream	1 toothbrush
1 tooth powder	1 sewing kit

The food items were not actually delivered to the individual prisoners but were placed in the mess hall where they were used to augment meals for all of the men. The sewing kits contained small scissors that were used to cut more than just fabric or thread. They also served as hair clippers and razors since not enough razor blades were received to keep the men clean shaven. Most of the prisoners kept their beards short with scissors.

During 1944, the Japanese were defeated in numerous Pacific island battles and suffered heavy troop losses. Officers of the Japanese Military Headquarters in Tokyo apparently were disturbed by a communiqué from the US State Department concerning Japan's war crimes against prisoners of war. In an August message transmitted to all Japanese prison camp commanders (and intercepted and decoded by the Allies), the Japanese Vice Minister of War explained methods for disposing of prisoners in times of urgency. That was generally considered to be anytime there was a danger of the prisoners being found by Allied forces. The Japanese message authorized disposal of prisoners by the following methods:

(a) Whether they are destroyed individually or in groups, or however it is done, with mass bombing, poisonous smoke, poisons, drowning, decapitation or what, dispose of them as the situation dictates.

(b) In any case it is the aim not to allow the escape of a single one, to annihilate them all, and not to leave any traces.[4]

The American campaign to recapture the Philippines began in October 1944 when American forces invaded Leyte. Although the prisoners did not immediately learn of the campaign, it soon became evident during the construction of the airfield that the Americans had returned to the Philippines.

One morning the men saw what appeared to be a high-flying American reconnaissance plane. It returned each day for several days, and then the prisoners were saddened to see it being shot down by a large number of what they assumed to be Japanese fighter planes flying out of Neilson Field. But they soon realized that the fighter planes were American, and that the reconnaissance plane they had seen destroyed was Japanese. A large number of Japanese fighter aircraft rose to meet the American fighters and an air battle ensued—which the prisoners watched in amazement. They were delighted to see all of the Japanese aircraft shot down. During the aerial display, the Japanese guards sought the shelter of the trees along the creek bed, but the Americans remained in the open where they could see it all!

"Boy, I wish I could be flying one of our planes right now," Clarence said. Some of the other prisoners expressed the same desire.

Then American bombers appeared and the men could see that they were bombing Neilson Field and the harbor area extensively. What a great day. The American prisoners were then taken to the prison compound area and were never returned to the landing field.

For some prisoners in other camps, the Americans' return to the Philippines meant that liberation was near. But for Clarence and the others with him, it simply meant the beginning of another, and even more terrible, phase of imprisonment.

ENDNOTES

1. Company-grade officers are commissioned officers holding the rank of second lieutenant, first lieutenant, or captain. Field-grade officers are senior officers holding the rank of major, lieutenant colonel, or colonel.

2. Prisoner names recorded by Clarence have been included in Appendix A. A selection of the poetry he recorded is included in Appendix B.

3. While at Cabanatuan, Clarence met a prisoner who had been a bookbinder in civilian life. The former bookbinder taught Clarence bookbinding skills, by which Clarence was able to bind his journal and his scriptures. To do this he used such pieces of Japanese newspapers and scraps of canvas shelter-halves as he was able to find. (A shelter-half is a piece of canvas material carried by each US soldier that, when combined with another similar piece, forms a two-man tent.)

4. Linda Goetz Holmes, *Unjust Enrichment: How Japan's Companies Built Postwar Fortunes Using American POWs* (Mechanicsburg, Pennsylvania: Stackpole Books, 2001). Journal of the Taiwan POW Camp HQ in Taihoku, Exhibit "O" in Doc. No. 2687, http://www.warbirdforum.com/murder.htm.

Chapter 10

The "Hell Ships"

From the time Pearl Harbor was attacked, Clarence was confident that Japan would be defeated. Early in his confinement he believed the prisoners would be liberated in a matter of months. As the months grew into years, he remained convinced of a coming liberation, although he could not estimate when that would be. "I have faith in God and in our country and I know our boys will be here to get us soon," he would say. He assumed that he and the other prisoners would be there in the Philippines to welcome them.

But he was soon to learn that the Japanese had plans to remove all prisoners from the Philippines who were capable of performing work for them in Japan or elsewhere. The Japanese military ordered that all "able-bodied" men be moved; "and as one source describes 'able bodied' meant any man who could stand."[1] Thus began Clarence's experience aboard one of the Japanese "hell ships."

"Hell ships" were freighters used to transport prisoners. Because they were unmarked, Allied aircraft and submarine crews had no way of knowing that they contained prisoners of war, and many were damaged or sunk and their passengers and crews drowned.[2] An estimated 22,000 American prisoners aboard these ships perished at sea by "friendly fire" because the

Japanese refused to fly the Red Cross flag required by the rules of the Geneva Convention,[3] even though Japanese weapons transports often bore Red Cross markings.[4] But the ships were not called "hell ships" solely for that reason. It was also because of the horrors that the prisoners endured while aboard.

On or about October 1, 1944, Clarence was one of approximately 1,100 American prisoners marched through the streets of Manila toward the waterfront. Hundreds, perhaps thousands, of Filipinos lined the streets to watch, and Clarence observed that many of the Filipinos wore clean white shirts and trousers. That was a sight seldom seen by Clarence during the Japanese occupation of the Philippines, and he considered it a sign of respect for the Americans.

When the prisoners reached Pier 7 and looked toward the harbor, they saw just above the waterline dozens of hulls and masts of sunken ships, starkly revealing the extensive damage already inflicted on Japanese shipping by American bombs. As the men marched along the pier, they passed many Red Cross food packages intended for the prisoners but already broken into, no doubt by Japanese soldiers, with most of their contents removed. The prisoners were then loaded aboard the *Hokusen Maru* (北鮮丸[5]), an inter-island freighter used most recently to transport coal and horses. Coal and horse manure still covered the bottoms of the two cargo holds.

The following notice was posted in imperfect English on all prison ships:

REGULATIONS FOR PRISONERS
Commander of POW Escort
Navy of the Great Japanese Empire

I. The prisoners disobeying the following orders will be punished with immediate death:

a. Those disobeying orders to instructions.

b. Those showing a motion to antagonism by raising a sign of opposition.

c. Those disobeying the regulations by individualism

egoism, thinking only about yourself or rushing for your own good.

d. Those talking without permission and raising loud voices.

e. Those walking and moving without orders.

f. Those who carry unnecessary baggage in disembarking.

g. Those resisting mutually.

h. Those touching the boats material, wires, lights, tools, switches, etc.

i. Those showing action of running away from the room or boat.

j. Those climbing the ladder without permission.

k. Those taking more meal than given him.

l. Those using more than blankets.

II. Since the boat is not well equipped and inside being narrow, food being scarce and poor you'll feel uncomfortable during the escort time on the boat. Those losing patience and disordering the regulations will be punished for the reason of not being able to escort.

III. Be sure to finish "nature's call." Evacuate the bowels and urine before embarking.

IV. Meal will be given twice a day. One plate only to one prisoner. The prisoners called by the guard will give out meal as quick as possible and honestly. The remaining prisoners will stay in their places quietly and wait for your plate. Those moving from their places, reaching for your plate without order will be heavily punished. Same orders will be applied to handling plates after meal.

V. Toilet will be fixed in four corners of the room, the buckets and cans will be placed, when filled up a guard will appoint a prisoner. The prisoner called will take the buckets to the center of the room. The buckets will be pulled up by the derrick to be thrown away. Toilet paper will be given. Everyone must co-operate to make the sanitary. Those being careless will be punished.

VI. The navy of the Great Japanese Empire will not try to punish you all with death. Those obeying all rules and regulations and delivering the action and purpose of the Japanese Navy; co-operating with Japan in constructing the "New Order of the Greater Asia" which leads to the world peace, will be well treated. The Great Japanese Empire will rise to Govern the World.

END[6]

北 鮮 丸

Japanese prison ship *Hokusen Maru. Abel Ortega Jr. Collection.*

The 1,100 prisoners were loaded into the two holds. In Clarence's hold, they entered by crawling through a three-by-five-foot overhead hatch and then descending a small ladder. Clarence noticed that John Cotten, with whom he had worked on the Las Pinas project, was among the prisoners in his hold, and the two men pushed their way toward each other.

Clarence said, "Well, John, it's good to see you again, although I wish it were under better circumstances."

"So do I. I wish our ship was going home instead of to Japan. I feel worse and worse, Rosie."

Clarence was glad to have John as a companion except that he couldn't really wish this trip on anyone.

As more men joined them, those already in the cargo hold were forced to move to the rear. Their sweating bodies were compressed so that no one could stand comfortably. The heavy wooden hatch cover was then dropped in place, leaving the men below in total darkness. The hold was completely shut off from outside air, and the stench of the manure and closely crowded bodies was nauseating.

The men were told that they could expect to be in Japan in eleven days. However, they remained in the harbor three or four days before even getting under way. Theirs was one ship of a larger convoy. Some prisoners felt that the Japanese intended American forces to sink their vessel inasmuch as it was not marked as a prison ship. And in fact, as noted, many prison ships did meet that fate. But Clarence correctly reasoned that the Japanese wanted them to reach Japan to be used as slave labor.

At first, because there was no room to lie down or even to sit, each man had to sleep in a standing position. But after four or five days, more room became available. This was partly because some men fashioned hammocks from blankets and hung them on the sides of the bulkheads, thus freeing up some of the floor space, but principally because men were dying. Each morning the surviving prisoners checked those around them. The bodies of those who had died during the night were hoisted topside to be dropped over the side of the ship.

The hold's hatch cover was removed from time to time, allowing at least some light and fresh air to enter. Prolonged periods of darkness contributed to the men's feelings of terror and helplessness, and some became insane.

While the Japanese convoy was sailing up the west coast of Luzon, American submarines sank most of the ships. But Clarence's ship was spared and continued on its way toward Hong Kong. The prisoners deep in the cargo holds heard the sounds of many American attacks and knew that if their ship sank, they could not escape. During one attack, a prisoner who had been in the Navy was heard to say, "I think we've been 'pinged' by one of our subs, but the sub commander just doesn't think this ship is worth sinking." Clarence didn't know whether that was true, but if it was, he was grateful.

Most of the men in the hold were young and unmarried. All were sick and starving. Suffering adversity together can be a bonding process, albeit an unwanted one. But as sick as Clarence was, John Cotten was sicker still. One night, as they sat next to each other in the darkness, Clarence heard John call out softly, "Mother, Mother . . ." Clarence put his arms around John's shoulders to comfort him, but by morning John had passed away. Clarence could not help crying. He was allowed to go up on deck to say a prayer before John's body was dropped into the sea. Clarence saved John's dog tags and a few small personal items.

The ship's freshwater pumps were inoperative, so the prisoners received barely enough water to remain alive. The little rice they received was pressed into small balls and placed in a bucket which was lowered into the hold. In the past, most of the prisoners had owned a "quan" can, which was a term for any kind of tin can or other metal container used to hold the edible plants or other food one might forage. But by this time the quan cans were gone.

Their only toilet facilities were five-gallon buckets lowered by a cable from the overhead hatch. Clarence recalled only one such bucket, but there may have been more. When a bucket was full, it was hoisted up through the hatch to have its contents dumped overboard. Sometimes the men in charge of the dumping were careless and some of the contents spilled into the hold on the prisoners. Sometimes the bucket was too full or the men simply couldn't reach it before having to go. And sometimes they just defecated, urinated, and vomited where they were. Those with dysentery had little choice.

When the journey began, the floor was covered with coal and horse manure. But to that was now added human feces, urine, and vomit. No one could be clean. Their clothing, their hair, their skin became foul and disgusting. There was no toilet paper, and the little water they received was needed for drinking and could not be spared for cleansing or hygiene purposes.

Fearing an epidemic when they arrived in Hong Kong harbor on October 11, some of the Japanese guards pooled their money and purchased a small quantity of buckets from Chinese merchants aboard small *sampans*[7] and distributed them among the prisoners to collect human waste. While in the harbor, a few prisoners at a time were allowed to be on deck for five minutes or so, and when it was Clarence's turn he was heartened to see an American B-24 bomber apparently returning from a raid. The B-24 dropped a single bomb and briefly strafed the harbor.

From Hong Kong they sailed north, finally reaching Takao, Formosa (Taiwan) on November 9,[8] 39 days after boarding the ship for an "eleven-day trip" to Japan—and they had not yet reached Japan. On docking in Takao, they noticed many sunken ships and bombed-out port facilities.

Clarence had many harsh and terrifying experiences as a prisoner of war, but he recalled his time aboard the *Hokusen Maru* as the worst. Conditions aboard the ship were so bad that the Japanese, now even more fearful of an epidemic, had the prisoners unloaded and deloused. Their clothing was boiled and they were taken to a school site now known as the Inrin Temporary Camp[9] where they

Inrin Temporary Camp, where Clarence Bramley and some 500 fellow prisoners spent two months while en route from the Philippines to Japan, 1944–45. *National Archives.*

remained for about nine and one-half weeks. Clarence remembers moving piles of rocks from one side of the schoolyard to the other.

The school was on a hillside, but the surrounding trees and vegetation made it impossible to see the homes around it. Clarence witnessed two air raids there. After the first raid, the Japanese burned the vegetation to create a smoke screen over the valley. But by the next day the smoke had cleared and the second raid occurred. The vegetation having been destroyed by fire, the prisoners could now see the surrounding homes. During that second air raid, some of the low-flying American air crews recognized the prisoners as Americans and waved to them. The guards retreated inside the school while the prisoners remained outside cheering their airmen on.

In Taiwan, Clarence was sent on a work detail to another camp housing British prisoners. During a rest period there, he sat on a log and read from his pocket New Testament. A nearby Japanese guard sat down beside him and in broken English instructed Clarence to read some verses aloud. Clarence did. The guard then said, "If America is supposed to be a Christian nation, why doesn't it act like one?"

Clarence does not recall how or even if he responded.

On January 12, 1945, the prisoners were marched into town where they were placed on a train to Takao, riding in coaches rather than boxcars. On the following day they were ordered to board the *Melbourne Maru* (めるぼるん丸), a somewhat larger and cleaner vessel than the one that had brought them to Taiwan. Again they were placed in a cargo hold, but it was roomier than the first and

The Melbourne Maru (めるぼるん丸). *Abel Ortega, Jr. Collection.*

the food sometimes included leftovers from other ships' passengers.

The weather became colder as they traveled north and the prisoners only had tropical clothing, and very little of that. So whereas they had suffered earlier from the heat, they now began to suffer from the cold. They stopped briefly in Shanghai and finally, on January 23, 1945, docked in the port of Moji on the northern tip of the Japanese island of Kyushu. Their "eleven-day" voyage from Manila Harbor to Japan had taken nearly four months.

Clarence Bramley's journal (above) shows an entry written on the back of cigarette packages explaining that his account of the journey from Manila to Taiwan was written at the request of the Japanese military. *Bramley Collection.*

ENDNOTES

1. Chad N. Proudfoot, "Hellships of World War II," *West Virginia Division of Culture and History,* copyright 2014, accessed December 17, 2014, http://www.wvculture.org/history/wvmemory/vets/hellships.html.

2. On one such ship, the *Junyo Maru* (順陽丸), of 5,620 POWs aboard, approximately 4,720 died when the ship was sunk.

3. Major Richard M. Gordon, "Remarks at the Manila American Cemetery," Ft. Bonifacio, Makati, Manila, Philippines (April 2, 2002).

4. "The Hell Ships," *Bataan Corregidor Memorial Foundation of New Mexico,* accessed December 17, 2014, http://www.angelfire.com/nm/bcmfofnm/hellships/hellships.html.

5. My thanks to Professor Masakazu Watabe of Brigham Young University for his help verifying these Japanese language names.

6. "When and How to Kill American POWs, Japanese Rules on Hellships," accessed January 10, 2007, www.west-point.org/family/adbc/stories_files/regulations.htm (site discontinued). See also "Regulations for Prisoners," accessed December 9, 2014, http://www.britain-at-war.org.uk/WW2/Hell_Ships/html/regulations_for_prisoners.htm.

7. *Sampans* were Chinese boats from twelve to fifteen feet long, usually covered with a house, and sometimes used as a permanent habitation on coastal and inland waters.

8. Scholars have suggested arrival dates between Oct. 24 and Nov. 11, 1944. Bramley's date is found in his contemporaneous journal.

9. Bramley's journal identifies the camp as "Inringai, Taiwan." The name "Inrin Temporary Camp" was coined by Michael Hurst MBE, Taiwan POW Camps Memorial Society, http://www.powtaiwan.org.

Chapter 11

JAPAN

A light snow was falling when the prisoners arrived in Moji. The following morning they were transported by ferry about a mile across the Kammon Straits to the port city of Shimonoseki, located on the southern end of the Japanese main island of Honshu. When they arrived, they were placed in a large warehouse they called "the icehouse" because it was so cold. They had begun their journey in the tropics wearing only the lightest clothing and they were now much farther north in mid-winter. They had no thermometer, but the men knew the temperature was below freezing. They huddled together for three days in the hope of retaining body heat, but still, one of the men froze to death.

On the morning of January 27, they were put on a train for the one-day trip to Tokyo. While waiting for the train to leave, one of their guards identified Clarence and his companions to Japanese civilian onlookers, who taunted the prisoners until the train departed. Shades were drawn over the windows of the train, but the prisoners could see around the shades' edges scenes of extensive burning and destruction, presumably from American air raids. Before arriving in Tokyo, a guard ordered the shades raised and proudly pointed out Mount Fuji as they passed by.

In Tokyo, each prisoner was given a blanket and an overcoat. They then boarded another train to continue their northward journey. Unlike the first train, this train's windows were left uncovered.

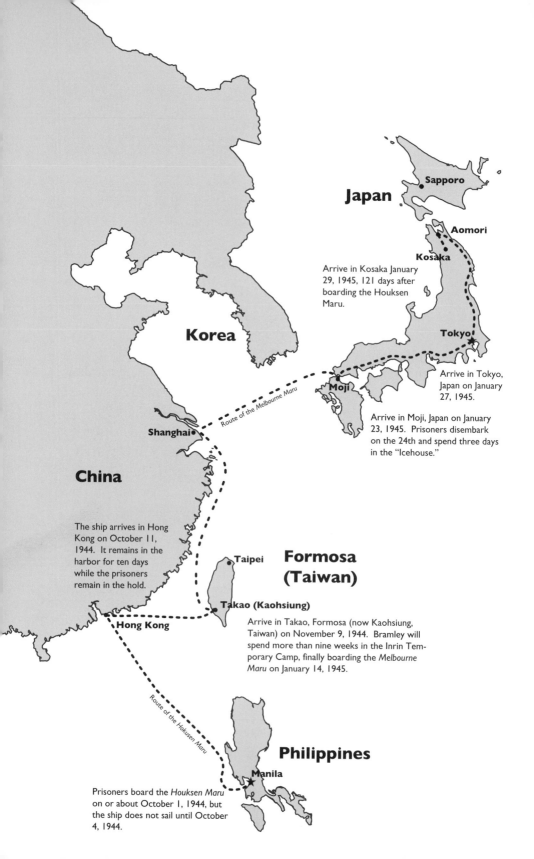

Japan

Sapporo

Aomori

Kosaka

Arrive in Kosaka January 29, 1945, 121 days after boarding the Houksen Maru.

Korea

Tokyo

Arrive in Tokyo, Japan on January 27, 1945.

Moji

Arrive in Moji, Japan on January 23, 1945. Prisoners disembark on the 24th and spend three days in the "Icehouse."

Route of the Melbourne Maru

Shanghai

China

The ship arrives in Hong Kong on October 11, 1944. It remains in the harbor for ten days while the prisoners remain in the hold.

Taipei

Formosa (Taiwan)

Takao (Kaohsiung)

Arrive in Takao, Formosa (now Kaohsiung, Taiwan) on November 9, 1944. Bramley will spend more than nine weeks in the Inrin Temporary Camp, finally boarding the *Melbourne Maru* on January 14, 1945.

Hong Kong

Route of the Hokusen Maru

Philippines

Manila

Prisoners board the *Houksen Maru* on or about October 1, 1944, but the ship does not sail until October 4, 1944.

After yet another change of trains, the prisoners arrived on the night of January 28 in the city of Aomori at the northern end of Honshu Island, where they were welcomed by more taunts from Japanese civilians. Half of the group remained in Aomori while the others, including Clarence, again changed trains. They traveled for several hours by narrow gauge railroad across the valley to the smelter town of Kosaka, arriving shortly before dawn on January 29, 1945. Those who survived would remain there until the war's end.

View of Kosaka prison camp with copper smelter in the background, 1945. *National Archives.*

At Kosaka they were marched in the snow from the station, through the town, and on to a camp on a hillside opposite the smelter. They were housed in wooden buildings, some single story and some a story and a half, with covered walkways leading from one building to another. Between each building was an outhouse that, though primitive, was a welcome improvement over the slit trenches of the Philippines. A high wood fence surrounded the entire area.

The snow continued to fall and was so deep on the ground that the men could not go outside the wooden buildings. Finally, after being snowed in for over two months, the prisoners were able to exercise on the surface of the snow, which was as high as the eves of the barracks.

When the snow melted, the men commenced work at the smelter. Prisoners from other areas soon brought the camp population to

Another view of the copper smelter at Kosaka, 1945.
National Archives.

340 men. Most were American, but some were from the United Kingdom, Holland, and Java. There were three work shifts per day at the smelter, as well as other special work details. Groups of ten to twenty men were also assigned to gather *fugi*, a plant similar in appearance to rhubarb but poisonous until dried and pickled. The Japanese used it in soup.

Except for the overcoat he received in Tokyo, the only clothing ever issued to Clarence while a prisoner was a set of Philippine issue denims he received at Camp O'Donnell, a G-string and a pair of shoes he received later while still in the Philippines, and a pair of replacement shoes he received while at the Inrin Temporary Camp. Because of his fair complexion, he felt compelled to make his set of denims last indefinitely and he patched them often. At Kosaka, the Japanese ordered the ranking American officer, Army Captain Thomas Walker Davis, to designate one prisoner to be a shoe repairman and another to be a tailor. Because Clarence had so often been seen sewing patches, he was designated the camp tailor. He was given the use of a small treadle (foot-powered) sewing machine.

Some of the Japanese officers and even a few of the enlisted men were sympathetic to the prisoners, more so than at any of the camps in the Philippines. A guard who was the official camp interpreter said he had lived in the United States before the war. He was familiar with the southwestern United States and he and Clarence talked often. "My commanding officer has informed me," he once confided to Clarence, "that after the Japanese defeat the Americans, I will become the mayor of Phoenix."

"I wouldn't count on it," Clarence replied.

Atomic cloud over Hiroshima. *National Archives.*

Chapter 12

BOMBS AND SURRENDER

Unknown to the prisoners in Prisoner of War Camp No. 8 in Kosaka, Japan, by mid-1945 the Allied forces were poised to attack Japan itself. At great cost they had advanced relentlessly across the western Pacific, and had finally taken the islands of Iwo Jima and Okinawa, which would provide bases from which to launch air strikes and an invasion against the Japanese home islands. But taking them had come at a high price. On Okinawa alone, 110,000 Japanese died, and American losses totaled 20,195 dead and 55,162 wounded. The Japanese had expected to lose both campaigns but were determined to inflict as many Allied casualties as possible in the process. They did not intend to surrender.

Former "Top Secret" documents, now declassified, reveal the Allied plans to invade Japan itself. The plans were finalized during the spring and summer of 1945 and called for two massive operations. The first, code-named "Operation Olympic," was to commence on November 1, 1945, with heavy naval and aerial bombardment followed by fourteen Army and Marine divisions conducting an amphibious assault on heavily defended Kyushu, the southernmost of the Japanese home islands. This was to be followed four months later by "Operation Coronet," with some 22 or more divisions landing on the main island of Honshu. The goal was to obtain Japan's unconditional surrender.

American military leaders anticipated that in an invasion of

Japan American casualties would be high. Admiral William Leahy foresaw more than 250,000 on Kyushu alone. General MacArthur's intelligence chief, General Charles Willoughby, estimated over a million for both operations and considered his estimate to be conservative. There would be even more enemy casualties as well, both military and civilian. On May 25, the US Joint Chiefs of Staff approved the invasion plans.

The United States had been secretly working on a new weapon, an atomic bomb, and a test code-named "Trinity" was successfully completed on July 16. The following day, President Truman, who was attending a conference in Potsdam, occupied Germany, was informed of the successful test and approved the invasion plans. The United Nations then issued the Potsdam Proclamation calling on Japan to surrender unconditionally. Three days later, on July 20, the Japanese government refused.

Prime Minister Winston Churchill, President Harry S. Truman, and Marshal Joseph Stalin at Potsdam Conference, 1945. *National Archives.*

A Japanese national slogan was "One Hundred Million Will Die for the Emperor and Nation."[1] Japanese radio broadcasts announced that Japan had closed all schools and had mobilized its schoolchildren. Civilians were being armed, caves were being fortified and underground defenses were being built. *Kamikaze* (suicide) aircraft and pilots were being assembled for the purpose of resisting an anticipated Allied invasion. Approximately 28 million Japanese civilians had become part of the National Volunteer Combat Force. *Kamikaze* pilots were looked on by the Japanese as "hero-gods," and boys publicly announced their ambition to grow up to become such.[2] There is little doubt that in the invasion many civilians would die in some form of combat or would commit suicide. A study done for US Secretary of War Henry Stimson's staff by William Shockley projected that an invasion would result in five to ten million Japanese deaths.[3]

For several months, the United States had dropped more than 63 million leaflets across Japan warning civilians of likely air raids. The leaflets, which urged the population to evacuate their cities and petition the emperor to end the war, appear to have pertained to American firebombing but it is disputed whether any pertained explicitly to an atomic attack.

On August 6, a Boeing B-29 superfortress bomber,[4] piloted by Colonel Paul Tibbets of the US Army Air Forces and dubbed "Enola Gay" after Tibbets's wife, left the island of Tinian headed for Hiroshima, Japan. It carried the first atomic bomb to be used in combat, code-named "Little Boy." The single bomb was more destructive than could have been imagined. It destroyed the city. According to figures published in 1945, 66,000 people were killed as a direct result of the blast, and 69,000 were injured in varying degrees.[5]

Colonel Paul W. Tibbets Jr., pilot of the "Enola Gay," the B-29 superfortress bomber that dropped the atomic bomb on Hiroshima, waves from his cockpit before takeoff, August 6, 1945. *National Archives.*

A second atomic bomb was dropped on the city of Nagasaki on August 9. The bomb, known as "Fat Man," was even more powerful than the first but resulted in fewer casualties and less damage because Hiroshima was on flat terrain, whereas Nagasaki lay in a small valley.

Some researchers have determined that actual casualties exceeded those estimates: "The real mortality of the atomic bombs that were dropped on Japan will never be known. The destruction and overwhelming chaos made orderly counting impossible. It is not unlikely that the estimates of killed and wounded in Hiroshima

Hiroshima business district days after atom bombing, on or about September 8, 1945. *National Archives.*

(150,000) and Nagasaki (75,000) are over conservative."[6]

On August 15, Emperor Hirohito announced publicly that he was willing to surrender, although some of his military commanders objected and offered temporary resistance. Some observers continue to assert that the Hiroshima and Nagasaki bombings were unnecessary in that Japan would have surrendered even without them. That appears unlikely.

An Allied correspondent stands in a sea of rubble in Hiroshima on September 8, 1945.
(*AP Photo/Stanley Troutman.*)

ENDNOTES

1. "How the Atomic Bomb Saved 4,000,000 Lives," *Omaha World Herald*, November, 1987, Davis.

2. Robert Sherrod, History of Marine Corps Aviation in World War II," (Washington: Combat Forces Press), 273.

3. Richard B. Frank, *Downfall: The End of the Imperial Japanese Empire* (New York: Random House, 1999).

4. The B-29 was a large and advanced US bomber. Among its new features, it had a pressurized cabin and remote-controlled machine gun turrets. Its name, "Superfortress," was derived from that of its predecessor, the B-17 "Flying Fortress," both of which were manufactured by Boeing.

5. The Manhattan Engineer District (June 29, 1946), *The Atomic Bombings of Hiroshima and Nagasaki*, Project Gutenberg Ebook, 3.

6. "Hiroshima and Nagasaki Death Toll," *Children of the Atomic Bomb*, a research website project developed by Dr. James N. Yamazaki, UCLA professor emeritus of pediatrics, together with the UCLA Asian American Studies Center. (Last modified October 10, 2007, accessed June 24, 2014, http://www.aasc.ucla.edu/cab/200708230009.html.)

Chapter 13

Parachute Drops and a Flag

Nearly a month passed before the prisoners in Kosaka Camp No. 8 learned of the bombings of Hiroshima and Nagasaki. But as far back as June they had begun to hear the obvious sounds of air raids in the distance. The men who worked in the smelter also heard from their Japanese guards that the prisoners might be going home soon. From this they surmised that the Americans were winning the war. For the first time since the war began, Clarence was able to obtain some paper to use as he wished and he began to write in a single document a series of separately dated letters to his parents, not knowing when or if he might be able to mail it, but believing that the opportunity would come.

The opportunity did come, and his parents retained the document until their deaths. What follows are portions of those letters:

Sunday, 8:00 p.m., August 5, 1945

Prisoner of War Camp No. 8

Kosaka, Japan

Dearest Mother and Dad,

I find myself at a loss for written words as I start this letter to you, who are nearest and dearest to my heart and always in my thoughts. I have been going to start this letter for some time, in fact I have actually written several first pages, but the written word seemed too inadequate for the thoughts and feeling of my heart. I feel that, the Good

Lord permitting, by adding a bit now and then, that it should not be unreasonably long before I can send this letter to you.

I just stepped outside for a breath of air and it is a beautiful Sabbath night after a nice day. The heavens are covered with stars, those same stars which you too enjoy, thanks to the Creator, our Good Lord. Oh that I could get the thoughts which are in my heart to flow in words from this pen.

We have been in Japan a bit over six months now. We have been greatly blessed here, as during all this period of war and imprisonment I have had a camp job all the time we have been at this camp. I am a camp tailor. It is a fine job, and at a later writing, I will give you a more detailed picture of our life here. My thoughts are rather mixed up, hence the rambling. It seems a bit difficult to get into the swing of letter writing again, but my thoughts are always with you and ever will be. I am looking forward to, and praying humbly for the day when, Lord willing, we will be joined together again.

Before closing this short beginning, I must bear my testimony to you, whom I love the most and owe more than I can ever repay, to the truthfulness of the Gospel of our Lord and Savior, Jesus Christ. . . . I pray that I might be given strength always to do His will and to live the life you would have me live, that I might, Lord willing, be privileged to be joined with you all again, furthering His work here on earth.

Until a later writing, when I hope to have my thoughts more in line, I remain your ever-loving son,

Clarence

Goodnight and God bless you all. My regards to all.

XXXOOO

Thursday, 7:00 p.m.

August 9, 1945

Dear Folks,

Here it is Thursday. The week has passed pretty fast it seems. I am just fine myself and I sincerely hope you are the same. We had quite a bit of rain today. It is the first rain we have had in more than a week or so now. We also had three air raids today. We have had several air raids here in the past two months and they are becoming more frequent now. As yet, we have seen no American planes, although many of our fellowmen here saw them in great numbers over Yokohama and Tokyo before they came up here. Good Lord willing, I hope it will be over soon. I have just returned from tinko (roll call) and am about to retire for my nightly foray with the fleas (we have plenty of them here now). They are a nuisance. We have 344 men here in the camp—150 of us from the Philippines came here in January. One hundred Dutchmen came up from Kawasaki (near Tokyo) the first of April, and 100 Americans, including a few Englishmen, came from Yokohama in May. Both the Dutch and the last Americans to come up here have been in Japan since early in the war. Our boat trip from the Philippines to Taiwan, where we spent two months, was a nightmare. Our trip from Taiwan to Japan was much better. The Yanks (God bless 'em) ran us out of both places. It was a real thrill to see them take over. I think they have us cornered now, too, as the Nips have no place else to move us. It was a bit of a trial coming from the tropics into the worst winter in forty years here, but we managed somehow, thanks to the Good Lord. We have lost seven of our bunch since we have been here, the last fellow died last Sunday after eating poisonous berries while on a green hunt [a search for edible grass or weeds, usually for making soup.] It has started to rain again and as I am a bit tired, I will bring this to a close for tonight. I will add more later.

I sincerely hope all is well at home. I hope Herb is okay, also the girls and children. My love to Grandma and you all. Regards also to all friends and relatives. I hope Knox is all right and still writes. God bless and keep you all. Until later then I am yours with love,

Clarie XXXOOO

Goodnight

Friday, 8:30 p.m.

August 10, 1945

Hello, Mom and Dad,

We have all learned a greater appreciation of the simpler and smaller things here. I won't deal much with our food here. It is a bit short, but the Good Lord has always seen us through, and POW's can't be choosers. . . .

Our work is going along okay. We ran out of machine thread today and, as there is no more available, we are going to do hand sewing tomorrow. The men here work in a smelter. There are three eight-hour shifts and two day crews working. The work would not be too bad if the food were not so short, but by the help of the Lord we will carry on. Lord willing, it shouldn't be long now. . . .

Saturday, 6:30 a.m.

August 18, 1945

Dearest Mother and Dad and rest,

. . . The night before last the fellows brought in a rumor to the effect that in three days the war would be over. Now we have had all kinds of rumors through our confinement, and although it is approaching that time, it seemed a bit hard to swallow. Upon waking during the night though, one noticed that the lights, which have been dimmed and turned out from 9:30 on, had been left on all night, most unusual in face of all the recent air raids. A ration detail came in from town with the report [that] hostilities had ceased and negotiations were under way. The war was over. The source, a Nip in charge of the slaughter house in town, had earlier in our time given us reliable news on German progress, so it sounded good. Then all kinds of rumors, news and what not came in with every detail from the shift workers in the plant. Just after noon, the Captain was told work at the plant would cease the following day, that we would rest and do no work other than keep ourselves supplied. . . . The fellows' morale really went up. We also received a 50 percent increase in chow, which is most unusual. We have also been getting a bit of blood, bones, guts and such which we have not had in sometime. Not many fellows got much sleep last night. . . .

Myself, as yet it seems so hard to comprehend. We have been here so long and yet all things seem to point to it. I might compare it in a way to one other time in my life, where there was loss and sorrow, this is joy and gain. Lennie's death was so hard to comprehend, it didn't seem real. So with this. Oh, I thank the Lord for all the wonderful blessings. Mother, without Him, it would have been a bit too much at times. I hope and pray that it is over, all the killing, destruction, hatred and all that war brings. I pray God to strengthen us all in building a better world than we have ever known, a world of righteousness.

Monday, 6:30 a.m.

August 20, 1945

Good Morning all,

. . . Now, I just returned from tinko, which turned out not to be tinko but an announcement by Captain Davis that there would be no tinko. Later we are to have a talk by the Japanese captain in charge of the camp who returned last night from Sendai headquarters after being called there two days previous. Captain Davis said he would probably tell us what we are waiting to hear and that from now on we would be more in charge of this camp than heretofore. Also, the doctors were informed last evening by the medical gocho (Japanese) they could have any and all medicine they needed to get the men well. So it is becoming more and more real all the time. . . .

Oh, a fellow just can't put into words the feelings that are in our hearts.

Captain Davis (second from right) and other Allied officers at Kosaka prison camp following the Japanese surrender. *Bramley Collection.*

The war was ending. There could be no real doubt about it. Clarence knew that he and the others who had survived months of combat and years of the horrible inhumanity of the prison camps did so because they never gave up hope in a final American victory and in liberation.

He also reflected on the lives that must have been lost and the damage, human and otherwise, that must have been inflicted around the world. He had personally witnessed some of it. Indeed, he had participated in it. A form of the old question returned. Had he acted well? He had tried to be true to his country and comrades. In the process, had he been true to his faith?

He had taken an oath to defend his country, the land of his birth, the land his parents chose. To do so had required that he be willing to give his own life, or take that of others, if necessary. There had been no dilemma, no decision to make, no need to resort to sophistry. The course he had to follow was self-evident. When your country, your family, or your comrades are threatened, you take whatever action is necessary to save them. You try to destroy your enemy, not because you hate him, but because you love your country, your way of life, and the people you have pledged to protect. And both Clarence's head and his heart affirmed that he did indeed love all of those. How he loved them. And maybe, just maybe, the world would now be a better place.

Wednesday, 7:45 a.m.

August 22, 1945

Good Morning all,

. . . The Japanese captain's speech was what we had been waiting for so long to hear. He told us that the whole world was at peace, that henceforth we would be a self-governing body in our camp here, and that henceforth we were guests of the Imperial government of Japan. It certainly is a wonder what a change this news has made. We have been completely reorganized and everything in camp is run in Army style— we are back in the U.S. Army. The men have perked up; the camp is kept 100 percent better and cleaner and is running much smoother

than under our former regime. Our food is much better than it was and there is no work other than our camp details and ration runs. We seem to be waiting here until facilities are available and arrangements for our departure are made. We hope to be on our way soon. It sure is swell to be back in the Army again. We have a bugler and it's all right to hear reveille, taps, and all the other calls, and although we have no flag, it's not hard to visualize the "Old Glory" fluttering in the breeze as we salute at reveille and retreat. . . .

The Lord has truly blessed us.

Although not in a position to do anything about it, and even though there was no flagpole in the camp, Clarence began to be troubled by the absence of an American flag.

Sunday, 11:00 p.m.

August 26, 1945

Good evening folks,

Boy things are getting better every day. Yesterday, Saturday, a new No. 1 thrill was registered when we saw our first American planes over our camp. They flew by the camp in the morning and returned at noon. After circling around a bit they came down and really gave us a grand show. There were twelve of them and they flew around for quite some time, coming down as low as possible, returning our shouts, cheers and delirious antics of joy with wing wagging and waving. Oh boy, it was really swell, surpassing all other thrills of our imprisonment. It was the first time I ever saw this bunch leave their chow for anything—voluntarily. . . .

Today dawned a beautiful Sabbath and where yesterday was superb, today was more so. Twenty-three planes from fighting squadron number one of the U.S. Navy returned this morning about 8:30 and after dropping a note to inform us of their intentions, commenced to drop bundles that contained emergency rations, magazines (late ones), medicines, shoes, cigarettes, and the latest newspapers from aboard their ship. It was wonderful. Boy, the Nips were completely snowed. The news in the paper was the latest and really enlightened us as to the real situation. . . . From the ship's news was learned, among many things, that tomorrow the first air-borne troops will invade and occupy Japan, beginning in the Tokyo area with General McArthur arriving Tuesday, the signing of the Armistice by Japan on the thirty-first, and most important to us individually, our immediate removal by plane and boat to the Philippines. What's more, there was a note in one of the boxes asking us what we needed and informing us how to signify what we needed—food, clothing or medicine. The sign of one panel was placed in the center of the compound for our number one need: food. Four planes came by shortly after noon and buzzed the camp a couple of times and wagged their wings. The pilots waved and took off. We are really looking forward to what the morrow may bring. I believe the show of the last two days has really convinced all, including the Nips, who is number one now. The Nip captain had the officers over to dinner, and the camp comes more and more under our control. The worm has turned. Man, the sight of these fliers really thrills a fellow, really makes one proud to know he is an American, a free one once again.

On September 2, 1945, formal surrender documents were signed aboard the battleship *USS Missouri*, bringing an official end to the war. General MacArthur signed on behalf of the United States and in attendance was a recently released former POW, General Wainwright.

Clarie's letter continued:

Thursday

September 6, 1945

Dearest Mother, Dad and all,

Well, a week has passed since I have written any word. What a week! To begin with, the short start on the last page was interrupted by a job of sewing that came up. That was the 30th of August, and thinking the 31st to be the official day for signing the final papers and taking over, a few of us fellows decided we should have a flag to hoist over the camp on this occasion. We started work on it after supper using colored chutes that had been used by the planes to drop our supplies. Four of the fellows [Charles Amos and three others] kept busy cutting stars and stripes, and I sewed them together. We worked all night and I finished the last hem and tie cords just before reveille. It was sure a real pleasure to make this flag. We surprised the camp and officers at

*reveille on unfurling it, but were unable to fly it as the final signing
was postponed till the 2nd, but everyone was very much impressed
and many of the fellows thanked me for our work. The Dutch and
British members had flags made. The next day, a Dutchman made
a Dutch flag, and I worked the night of the 2nd sewing the Union
Jack, which two of the British officers cut out and designed. We had
the official camp premiere of the flags at reveille the morning of the
third and the three flags now daily flutter from the top of the barracks
buildings here.[1]*

The officers and men in the camp had been hardened by years
of combat and imprisonment. Still, most of them cried with joy at
the sight of Old Glory.

ENDNOTES

1. The American flag made by Clarence Bramley, Charles Amos, and three other
prisoners is approximately 35 inches in height and 52 inches in width. It was
publicly displayed for more than five years at Brigham Young University and is
now in Bramley's possession.

Flag made in Kosaka prison camp. *Bramley Collection.*

Spectators and photographers await
the Japanese delegation on board the
USS Missouri in Tokyo Bay.
National Archives.

The Japanese delegation prepares to sign
surrender documents aboard the
USS Missouri, September 2, 1945.
National Archives.

General Douglas MacArthur signs as Supreme Allied Commander during
formal surrender ceremonies on the *USS Missouri* in Tokyo Bay. Behind
General MacArthur are Lieutenant General Johnathan Wainwright and
Lieutenant General A. E. Percival. *National Archives.*

US Navy personnel salute the departing Japanese delegation.
National Archives.

US Navy and Marine aircraft overfly the surrender proceedings.
National Archives.

Chapter 14

Parachute Drops Continue

Although conditions were now far better for the prisoners than at any time since their captivity began, they were still sick and weak. All were malnourished and had lost an extreme amount of weight. Clarence had suffered malaria, beriberi, dengue fever, sunstroke, blindness, and dysentery. In this he was not greatly unlike his fellow prisoners. Before the Bataan surrender he had weighed 185 pounds, but he had since lost over a hundred, making him now under 85 pounds. He was thrilled to be able to eat nourishing food again, and in his letter of September 6 to his parents, he wrote:

The past week has really been some stuff. To begin with, our fellow-men from the Navy continued dropping bundles of supplies to us daily until the 28th. The afternoon of the 28th, they flew over but didn't drop anything. Later in the afternoon two large four-motored planes appeared on the horizon, and as they came nearer [they] turned out to be B-29s and the Army took over. . . . It sure was the berries: food (including all kinds of canned goods, fruit, soups, vegetables, Type C and K rations), clothing (including shoes, complete uniforms, toilet accessories, soap), reading material, candy, gum, cigarettes, matches, things we haven't seen or had in years. In two drops this one B-29 gave us more clothing, soap and things of that nature than we have had issued in three and a half years under the Nips. The food things we haven't had since we left home, and more food for a three-day issue than the Nips have ever issued for double that number of months, excluding rice. In messages found in the boxes, we were told we would

Clarence Bramley (third from right, standing) and a group of Allied prisoners at Kosaka camp dressed in new clothes from parachute drops. *Bramley Collection.*

be supplied by air in this manner from now until we move. More than keeping their word, they returned the 30th with another big load that came down more successfully. It was here we received the colored chutes for our flag. They missed us a couple three days next time, and day before yesterday two of them came over and dropped four loads, sixty some odd chutes. Boy, we can give away gum galore, candy, books, complete clothing outfits for every man, two for most, from head to foot. It's sure swell to be able to eat without wondering if you'll have any for tomorrow.

Other B-29s and more supplies followed. Each parachute brought a 50-gallon drum filled with items the prisoners had longed for during their captivity. And each drop included a message from the bomber crew, all similar to this one received on the 31st:

August 31, 1945

Friday

Fellow Americans:

We have flown over 3,500 miles to bring you these supplies. We enjoy doing what we can to bring you aid and comfort. Look for us again. We hope we can all be back in the USA again soon.

Crew of B-29 "Slick Dick"

    (Commd) Capt. Edward M. Ware

    (Pilot) 2nd Lt. John E. Ussery

    (Bombardier) 1st Lt. John J. Janosko

    (Navigator) 2nd Lt. Richard N. Luzier

    (Radio Opr.) 1st Lt. Norris D. Beairo

    (Engineer) T/Sgt. Arthur J. Henery

    (Radio Opr.) Sgt. Harold J. Pickait

    (Cent. Fire Cont.) Sgt. Waring Lerdy

    (Rgt. Gunner) Sgt. Thomas J. Marshal

    (Lgt. Gunner) Sgt. Del C. Inman

    (Tail Gunner) Sgt. Nicholas Fosticrako

A.P.O.-234

500th Bomb. Grp., 882 Sqdn.

C/o Postmaster, San Francisco,

California

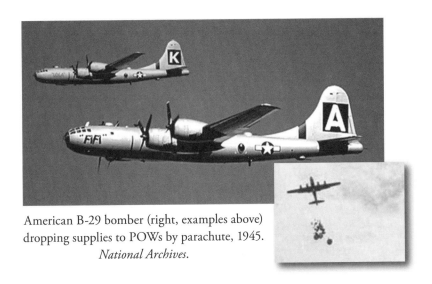

American B-29 bomber (right, examples above) dropping supplies to POWs by parachute, 1945. *National Archives.*

Death March Survivor Reported on Way Home

WORD has just been received by the mother of a survivor of the Bataan death march that he was "overwhelmed" by his liberation by the "good old Yanks," and will be on his way home soon.

Cpl. Clarence H. Bramley, 28, of the Army Air Corps landed in the Philippines only two weeks before war. Living through the losing battle of Bataan and the march of prisoners that took so many lives, he subsequently survived 40 months as a Jap captive.

Yesterday his parents, Mr. and Mrs. Herbert Bramley of 5564 Lewis Ave., received their first letter from him, and he wrote he is in "good health." The letter was dated Sept. 14 from Yokohama. He is a graduate of Wilson High School and entered the service in February, 1941.

The Bramleys have another son in the service, Herbert Jr., a lieutenant in the Air Force, who arrived home yesterday from Truax Field, Madison, Wis.

On September 13, Clarence boarded a Navy transport ship bound for Yokohama, the first leg of the long journey home. A sailor's cheerful voice called out, "Anybody here from Long Beach, California?"

Clarence became excited. "I am," he said.

Further conversation revealed that the sailor's name was Crandall. He was also from Long Beach and was a friend of Clarence's younger brother, Herb. Crandall volunteered to mail Clarence's letters to his parents, which were likely to arrive long before Clarence would. Clarence was to fly from Yokohama to Manila and sail from there to San Francisco. On October 13, Herbert and Ellen Bramley received another telegram from the Army adjutant general:

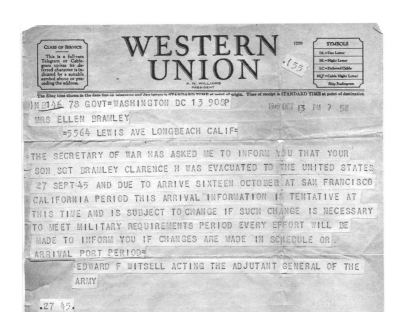

IN B146 78 GOVT=WASHINGTON DC 13 908P   1949 OCT 13 PM 7 58

MRS ELLEN BRAMLEY

=5564 LEWIS AVE LONGBEACH CALIF=

THE SECRETARY OF WAR HAS ASKED ME TO INFORM YOU THAT YOUR
SON SGT BRAMLEY CLARENCE H WAS EVACUATED TO THE UNITED STATES
27 SEPT 45 AND DUE TO ARRIVE SIXTEEN OCTOBER AT SAN FRANCISCO
CALIFORNIA PERIOD THIS ARRIVAL INFORMATION IS TENTATIVE AT
THIS TIME AND IS SUBJECT TO CHANGE IF SUCH CHANGE IS NECESSARY
TO MEET MILITARY REQUIREMENTS PERIOD EVERY EFFORT WILL BE
MADE TO INFORM YOU IF CHANGES ARE MADE IN SCHEDULE OR
ARRIVAL PORT PERIOD=

EDWARD F WITSELL ACTING THE ADJUTANT GENERAL OF THE
ARMY

.27 45.

127

Photo of Clarence and Herbert Bramley taken after the war.
Bramley Collection.

Chapter 15

HOME

By the time Clarence arrived in San Francisco, he had ballooned to 220 pounds. They were not "good" pounds, he said. He spent over three months in the Birmingham Army Hospital in Los Angeles recovering from the illnesses he had contracted as a POW, as well as his rapid weight gain. He found that his brother Herbert had also joined the US Army Air Forces, as the US Army Air Corps became known in 1941 (not to be confused with its later designation as the US Air Force, when it became a separate and independent branch of the armed forces in 1947), and had become a pilot, just as Clarence had hoped to be.

In fact, Clarence learned that he himself had passed the flight training examination taken four years earlier. But even though he had just been promoted to sergeant, he elected to leave the service. He received an Honorable Discharge on May 3, 1946. It was neither a difficult decision nor a fancy ceremony. By then, Clarence had been in the Army for five years, two months, and nineteen days, and he received $300 mustering out pay. No frills. In the end, becoming a flyer was not what counted most.

Clarence also learned that his old friend, Knox Kendall, with whom he had entered army service, had also been assigned to the Philippines, but did not actually arrive there. He was en route to the Philippines at the time of the attack on Pearl Harbor, and he was ordered back to the United States. From there he went to the Burma

Honorable Discharge issued to Clarence H. Bramley, May 3, 1946.
Bramley Collection.

theater of operations where he served during most of the war.

Clarence was able to find the address of John Cotten's parents and mailed John's dog tags and small personal items to them with a letter of sympathy. Unknown to Clarence at the time, John's father had already passed away. Later, Clarence received a letter of thanks from a heartsick Mrs. Cotten, and as he read it, he envisioned her tearfully and laboriously attempting to describe her feelings. A portion of her letter follows:

Did you know Johnnie when he received letter from me telling him about passing away of his father May 12/43. I have thought that letter was too much for him. At time we were all so worried. I was sad, lonely, sick and so very depressed I wrote letter to him every day telling him just what was on my heart so not knowing which letter he would receive (if any one of them). He received one and all others came back to me. But was afraid it was too much for him. That he just about gave up then. Tell me if you know.

Clarence, I know Johnnie was a Christian and his father knew he was. Johnnie professed Christ as his Savior when was about ten years old [and] *was baptized in* [the] *First Baptist Church.*

Clarence, worry about Johnnie was one thing that caused his father's death—he didn't believe he would come back. And I never gave him up . . .

I believe I know the day Johnnie got on the ship and I know when he was so very sick and when he passed away. . . . It was over a week in October 1, '44, that I heard Johnnie calling, "Mother, Mother." I heard him day and night; of course couldn't eat or sleep. Down deep in my heart and mind I knew something had happened but just couldn't give him up for I wanted him to come home to me so bad. . . .

And when a hometown boy was liberating all the prison camps when was about over, yet I couldn't believe it. He kept writing home, "Can't find John . . "

Would you be kind enough tell me more about his burial? About how many were buried in China Sea?

And remember your letters are so much to me and my family. So must say ByBy for now.

Your other Mom,

Mrs. Cotten

Clarence noted that the time Mrs. Cotten reported hearing Johnnie calling for her was at or about the same time that Johnnie, in Clarence's arms, actually did call for his mother just before passing away.

Clarence learned that his old girlfriend, Joyce Hayes, was divorced and he went to see her. Their meeting was friendly, but Clarence decided not to further a relationship with her. For some time Bryce Lilly had suggested that Clarence call on his sister,

Norma Jean Lilly, who was serving with the US Marine Corps at the El Toro, California, Marine Corps Air Station. She had enlisted on November 3, 1943, her twenty-first birthday. He met and married her in 1946. Clarence says it was love at first sight. When he first met Norma Jean, she asked why it had taken him so long (three months after his return to the United States) to see her. He wondered himself since while he was in the hospital, he was often able to obtain weekend passes. Shortly after their wedding, the following article was published in the Long Beach Press-Telegram:

> Three men who were together on the death march of Bataan in 1942 were on a wedding march together in 1946. The wedding was that of Clarence Bramley of Long Beach and Miss Norma Jean Lilly of Tacoma, early this month at the bride's home. The other two Bataan men who participated are Bryce Lilly, brother of the bride, who gave her away, and Kenneth Vick, best man.
>
> The three members of the 21st Pursuit Squadron in the Philippines were captured together by the Japanese. They were sent to separate camps, but found each other when liberated. Bramley came home to Long Beach and Lilly wrote that his sister was stationed at near-by El Toro with the women marines. He asked Bramley to visit her. After a second look Bramley wasn't looking at anyone else.
>
> The bride is the daughter of Mrs. Norman A. Lilly of Tacoma. The bridegroom is the son of Mrs. Herbert Bramley of Long Beach. After a honeymoon at Yellowstone [Park] and in Salt Lake City they will live here.

After his Army discharge, Clarence returned to laying linoleum. He took the civil service examination to become a firefighter for the city of Los Angeles and while awaiting the results, he received the following letter from General George Moore, the commanding general of the United States Army Forces in the Philippines. The general's letter referenced a letter from Aubrey Bissonnette that had described Clarence's sacrifices and good humor while a prisoner of war, attributes that had "kept many a sick man from going over the hill."

UNITED STATES ARMY
PHILIPPINES—RYUKYUS COMMAND
OFFICE OF THE COMMANDING GENERAL

APO 707

NOV 1 1947

Mr. Clarence H. Bramley
5564 Lewis Avenue
Long Beach 5, California, U.S.A.

Dear Mr. Bramley:

A letter has been received from Sergeant Aubrey F. Bissonnette, a former Prisoner of War, informing me of the outstanding services you rendered while a Prisoner of War to Prisoners of War, and to the cause of the United States, the Philippine Commonwealth and Allies during the recent war.

Since I believe you will appreciate having this letter, I have had copies made and am enclosing one of them for you.

I personally desire to express my appreciation for the splendid services you have rendered.

Sincerely,

GEO F. MOORE
Major General, U.S. Army
Commanding

1 Incl:

Copy of letter from Sergeant Aubrey F. Bissonnette

Letter dated November 1, 1947, from Major General Moore expressing appreciation for Clarence Bramley's service while a prisoner of war.
Bramley Collection.

After receiving notice that he had passed the civil service examination, in 1949 Clarence became a Los Angeles City firefighter. He and Norma Jean tried unsuccessfully to have children. They sought medical help but were informed by their physician that Clarence was incapable as a result of the diseases he had suffered in the prison camps. Still, they wanted a family, so they adopted and raised four children, Terrea Lee, Mona Annette, James Leonard, and Steven Glen.[1] They loved the children and each other. Clarence retired from the fire department in 1979 after more than thirty years of service. He remains an active member of The Church of Jesus Christ of Latter-day Saints. Norma Jean passed away in 1999 at the age of 76. Recently, Clarence found tucked away between the pages of a book at his home the following note in Norma Jean's handwriting:

> How gracious and kind God has been, an ever-living hand in our life, holding us together, healing hurts, giving us love and caring, lifting us above ourselves, making our lives worthwhile. Without Him we would be nothing.
>
> Marriage has been a terrific experience that goes on and on. All the joy, love and laughter, the sad times we have shared together, the hurts we have come through. Every day is something new we didn't plan on. Clarie gives me a balance, something to hold on to. I can't imagine life without him. The time has gone so fast, yet we still have each other. We still belong together. I'm just so glad for what we have.

When asked which of several pictures of Norma Jean and him he would like included in this account, Clarence said, "Any picture that has her in it would be wonderful."

ENDNOTES

1. James Leonard died in 1976 at the age of 20. Steven Glen died in 2002 at the age of 36.

Women Marines basic training class graduation, with Norma Jean Lilly in the second row, third from the left, January 1944. *Bramley Collection.*

Norma Jean Lilly (left) and three marine friends at Camp Lejeune, North Carolina, 1944. *Bramley Collection.*

Norma Jean Lilly, 1943, age 20. *Bramley Collection.*

Norma Jean Lilly in her Marine Corps uniform and Clarence Herbert
Bramley in his Army uniform just before their marriage in 1946.
Bramley Collection.

Clarence and Norma Jean Bramley in 1998, shortly before Norma
Jean's death. *Bramley Collection.*

Chapter 16

A Soldier's Faith

The loss of the Philippines was the largest single defeat of American forces in history. The American and Filipino troops who fought the Japanese in late 1941 and early 1942 fought bravely and superbly. But without food, ammunition, or medical supplies, their military commanders, Major General Edward King and Lieutenant General Jonathan Wainwright, sadly (but no doubt accurately) concluded that they had no alternative but to surrender.

King later said that during his entire time as a prisoner of war, he expected to be court-martialed at war's end because by surrendering his forces on Bataan, he had violated orders from General MacArthur, and later, orders from General Wainwright. But no court-martial was held and most of the Bataan survivors credit him with courageously saving their lives. Similarly, Wainwright, who also became a prisoner of war, anticipated a court-martial. Instead (over MacArthur's initial opposition), on the recommendation of General George C. Marshall, the Army's Chief of Staff, he received the Congressional Medal of Honor, the nation's highest military award.

MacArthur has received considerable criticism for his failure to attack Japanese aircraft on the island of Formosa, thus allowing them to attack Clark and Iba Fields and decimate the Far East Air Force on the first day of the war. While some facts remain in dispute, the following summary of events is widely accepted:

On December 8, 1941, in Manila, the Japanese were known

to have a large air force on Formosa, some 600 miles to the north. A previously approved US plan known as Rainbow 5 called for a US attack on Formosa in the event of war. According to Major

General Brereton's war memoirs, when he learned of the Pearl Harbor attack he proceeded to MacArthur's headquarters, arriving at 5:00 a.m. He tried to see MacArthur to urge an immediate air attack in accordance with the plan. Brigadier General Sutherland, MacArthur's chief of staff, told Brereton that MacArthur was in conference with Admiral Hart and could not be disturbed but that he, Sutherland, would relay the request to MacArthur. Brereton left.

Major General General Lewis H. Brereton, 1941. *National Archives.*

Half an hour later, MacArthur received a cable from Washington directing him to implement the Rainbow 5 plan immediately. Around 7:15 a.m., having received no approval for an air attack, Brereton returned to see MacArthur but was again refused by Sutherland, who told him that MacArthur said not to send planes to Formosa because the United States was not to "make the first overt act."[1]

Around 9:00 a.m. Brereton received a telephone call from General Arnold[2] in Washington directing him to get his planes in the air so they would not be caught on the ground like those at Pearl Harbor. Brereton then scrambled 36 P-40s and all but one of his B-17s to stay aloft until otherwise instructed. Brereton continued without success to try to see MacArthur. Finally, at approximately 9:45 a.m., MacArthur or Sutherland, or both, called Brereton directing him to send a photo-reconnaissance flight to Formosa to see if potential targets could be identified. If so, a bombing mission would follow that afternoon. Brereton then ordered all aircraft to land, fuel, arm, and prepare for the mission. It was after they landed and while they were on the ground preparing that the Japanese attack came.[3]

MacArthur's stated recollection of the facts was otherwise. In 1946 he issued a statement to the press denying that Brereton had called for a strike against Formosa. He said further that such a mission would have failed because of the inability to provide a fighter escort for the long flight, the fighter planes having a shorter range than the bombers.[4]

It is difficult to see how a strike against Formosa could have been considered a "first overt act." That description would more accurately apply to the Japanese attack against Pearl Harbor. Further, by 5:30 a.m. on December 8, MacArthur had received instructions to proceed with attacks consistent with Rainbow 5.

Heavy fog delayed for six hours the takeoff of any Formosa-based aircraft. While that fact should have been an advantage to the Americans (because had they attacked immediately they might have been able destroy the Japanese aircraft on the ground), the fog might also have made it difficult for the Americans to bomb effectively. Whether fighter cover for the bombers would have been required is also open to question. If the bombers had reached their Formosa target before the fog lifted, enemy fighters would probably not have yet been airborne, making American fighter cover unnecessary.

Some critics have expressed the belief that MacArthur simply dithered, not knowing what to do. Others have said that he may have believed the Philippines would remain neutral and so was reluctant to damage that neutrality. Having that same day attacked the US territories of Hawaii and Guam, it is unlikely that the Japanese intended to allow the Philippines, a US protectorate, to remain neutral.

For most, the criticism of MacArthur is justified, although for others, who is to blame remains an issue. In the early days of the war Americans were longing for good news and for a hero, and MacArthur seemed to satisfy that longing. He was not known to hide from publicity. Of course, he went on to be appointed General of the Army,[5] to lead the US forces to victory in the Pacific, and to become the primary leader of post-war Japan.[6]

The Bataan Death March and the ensuing treatment of Allied prisoners of war, all terrible atrocities, were undoubtedly due at least in part to the Japanese view that surrender was dishonorable; therefore, the POWs did not deserve better. This is illustrated in the last message of Japanese Lieutenant General Yoshitsugu Saito to the officers and men of his command on Saipan in 1944 wherein he ordered them to fight to their deaths. He recalled the essence of the *Bushido* warrior code which emphasized the duty of the *samurai* to give his life in service to his lord:

As it says in the *Senjinkun* (Battle Ethics), "I will never suffer the disgrace of being taken alive," and "I will offer up the courage of my soul and calmly rejoice in living by the eternal principle."[7]

"The Japanese 1941 field service code, with Imperial sanction, decreed that surrender was impermissible. Soldiers knew that if they were captured, they faced death upon returning home."[8] This would explain why so few Japanese were captured and so many were killed.[9] It would also explain why Japanese soldiers taken prisoner by the Americans were summarily executed by their Japanese brothers.

As noted earlier, Japan had not ratified the signing of the 1929 Geneva Convention rules. But the Japanese commanders knew that most of the prisoners on the March were in a pitiful state of health even before the march began. Lieutenant General Homma drove the marchers brutally under the burning sun, denying them food or water. Many died of sickness, thirst, and starvation while many more were killed by their guards because they were simply too weak to keep up. The same can be said of deaths in the camps. Clarence observed that "a lot of guys just gave up hope and died."

It has been reported that "more POWs died at the hands of the Japanese in the Pacific theater and specifically in the Philippines than in any other conflict to date. In Germany in WWII, POWs died at a rate of 1.2 percent. In the Pacific theater the rate was 37 percent. In the Philippines POWs died at a rate of 40 percent."[10]

At war's end, General Homma was charged with bombing Manila after it had been declared an open city, refusing quarter to the American troops on Corregidor, and allowing massive atrocities on the Death March and at O'Donnell, Cabanatuan, and other prison camps—all war crimes. In his defense, he claimed that he did not know of the atrocities until long after they had taken place. He was found guilty of all charges and was executed by a firing squad (which he requested over death by hanging) on April 3, 1946.

War crimes trial of Lt. Gen. Homma, held in Manila, 1946.
National Archives.

Clarence's account of the raping and killing of Filipino women by Japanese soldiers is similar to other accounts of atrocities against women throughout Southeast Asia. Although the Japanese government has not officially acknowledged such conduct, a former Japanese soldier, Yasuji Kaneko, admitted to the Washington Post that such things were common. He said that the women "cried out, but it didn't matter to us whether the women lived or died. We were the emperor's soldiers. Whether in military brothels or in the villages, we raped without reluctance."[11]

The apparent pleasure some Japanese soldiers derived from their cruelties may have stemmed from a misguided belief that theirs was the superior race and that all others existed only to do their will. Commenting on his experiences in China, a former Japanese Army officer, Uno Shintaro, said:

> Torture was an unavoidable necessity. Murdering and burying them follows naturally. You do it so you won't be found out. I believed and acted this way because I was convinced of what I was doing. We carried out our duty as instructed by our masters. We did it for the sake of our country. From our filial obligation to our ancestors. On the battlefield, we never really considered the Chinese humans. When you're winning, the losers look really miserable. We concluded that the Yamato [Japanese] race was superior.[12]

Clarence Bramley vividly recalls the brutality of his captors, but he also recalls the instances of kindness. "Some Japanese were bad and some were good, just like people everywhere," he states. "The officer who had me loaded on the cart to save me from being bayoneted, the guard who had cold water pumped on me to lower my fever, the sergeant who prevented ten of us from being executed, even the officer who apologized for striking me after he discovered that I wasn't responsible for the theft of the squid—all these were examples of man's regard for his fellowman."

While these good acts certainly do not balance out the willful starvation, torture, and death experienced by Allied forces in the Philippines and Japan, they do lead to the inescapable conclusion that in every culture there are at least some men of good will. Perhaps it is a hopeful sign that *Senjinkun* is rarely discussed in Japan today.

Clarence has often considered what gift he might give Aubrey Bissonnette to show his appreciation for what Bissonnette did to help him on the March. He finally concluded that no material thing he could give would be sufficient. "What do you do for a man who saved your life?" he asks. He then answers his own question, "You just thank him, remember him, thank the Lord for sending him, and be the best person you can be."

Throughout his captivity, Clarence continued to trust in a loving and merciful God. He tried to keep hope alive among his fellow prisoners. He inspired them by his example and encouragement, and with a flag that evoked tears of joy, a deep sense of gratitude, and a renewed confidence in the determination of the United States to care for her children.

Clarence credits his faith, his love for his family, and his devotion to his country for his ability to remain optimistic in the face of severe adversity. In a letter to his parents dated August 5, 1945—shortly before the war's end—he said,

> *I am humbly grateful for the bringing up you have given me, and though I can never repay, I sincerely pray that I might have the strength to be the man you would have me be. I am thankful to the Lord for the comfort, peace of mind and happiness that a knowledge of Christ brings, also for the care and protective guidance and innumerable blessings which have been poured upon myself and my fellowmen through these troubled times.*

Flag made in Kosaka prison camp. *Bramley Collection.*

ENDNOTES

1. On November 27, 1941, General George C. Marshall, US Army Chief of Staff, sent a message to Army commanders that if hostilities could not be avoided, the United States desired that Japan commit the first overt act. However, by 5:30 a.m. on December 8, MacArthur received a radiogram from Marshall advising that hostilities between Japan and the United States had begun and that MacArthur was to carry out the attacks assigned in Rainbow 5.

2. General Henry Harley "Hap" Arnold was an aviation pioneer and commanding general of all US Army Air Forces during World War II.

3. Robert C. Daniels, "MacArthur's Failures in the Philippines, December 1941–March 1942," copyright 2007, accessed Sept. 4, 2014, http://www.militaryhistoryonline.com/wwii/articles/macarthursfailures.aspx.

4. See ibid. Jennifer L. Bailey, *Philippine Islands: the U.S. Army Campaigns of World War II*, "Philippine Islands: 7 December 1941–10 May 1942," essay for US Army Center of Military History, with introduction by M. P. W. Stone, Secretary of the Army, p. 19–20, accessed September 4, 2014, http://www.history.army.mil/html/books/072/72-3/CMH_Pub_72-3.pdf. Mark Douglas, *MacArthur's Pacific Appeasement, December 8, 1941: The Missing 10 Hours*, (Bloomington, Indiana: Trafford Publishing, 2012).

5. "General of the Army" is a five-star rank not currently held by anyone. During and since World War II, the five-star rank (General of the Army or Admiral of the Fleet) has been held by only five persons in the Army: George Marshall, Douglas MacArthur, Dwight D. Eisenhower, Henry H. Arnold, and Omar Bradley; and four persons in the Navy: William D. Leahy, Ernest J. King, Chester W. Nimitz, and William F. Halsey. The rank is second only to "General of the Armies," a rank held by only two persons in US history: John J. Pershing and George Washington.

6. MacArthur was named Supreme Commander for the Allied Powers (SCAP) in post-war Japan, helping that nation to rebuild, to institute a democratic government, and to become an industrial power.

7. R. R. Keene, *Leatherneck Magazine*, June 2004, 30.

8. Jeff Kingston, "Impermissible surrender and its consequences," *The Japan Times*, April 10, 2005.

9. On July 9, 1944, while Japanese forces were being defeated in the battle of Saipan, General Saito, facing east, said, "Tenno Haika! Banzai!" ("Long live the Emperor!"), after which he drew his sword and committed *seppuku* by

disemboweling himself with his sword. R. R. Keene, *Leatherneck Magazine*, June 2004, 30.

10. "American Experience," *PBS*, accessed March 25, 2009, http://www.pbs.org/wgbh/amex/bataan/peopleevents/e_geneva.html.

11. Hiroko Tabuchi, the Associated Press, "Japan's Abe: No Proof of WWII Sex Slaves," *Washington Post*, Thursday, March 1, 2007.

12. Haruko Taya Cook & Theodore F. Cook, *Japan at War* (New York: New Press, 1993), 153.

Appendix A

OTHERS WHO SERVED

Clarence Bramley recorded names and addresses of some of his fellow POWs, including officers for whom he worked as an orderly, prisoners who attended church services with him, and others who became good friends. The following list of soldiers and civilians was extracted from his notebook verbatim to honor the men who served with him as prisoners of war. Hometown locations have been corrected for spelling where necessary. Ranks and unit affiliations were not recorded for all POWs. In some cases, soldiers provided alternative hometown locations. In a few cases, a soldier's name was recorded without a hometown.

Aldrich, Jack H.—Capitan, NM
Allen, Sherdie W.—Stowe, VT
Amos, Charles I.—Providence, RI
Anderson, Grubbs—Albuquerque, NM
Atkinson, J. C.—Eldorado, AR
Baclawski, Arthur M.—Cleveland, OH or Elephant Butte, NM
Becker, Harold C.—Maywood, IL
Bell, Robert N.—Oak Park, IL
Bell, Francis E.—Wellsville, KS and/or Miami, FL
Benson or Pomerene—AZ
Berkenboseh, Jan—Hoogeveen, The Netherlands
Berlanga, Martin—San Antonio, TX
Bila, A. George—Omaha, NE

Blanning, J. C. (Major) 26th Cav.—Colorado Springs, CO
Boolos, Demetri L.—Tulsa, OK
Braye, Paul W.—Salinas, CA
Brown, Earl R.—Albuquerque, NM
Bullock, Marvin C.—Jamestown, NY
Burns, Robert Glen—Shreveport, LA
Burris, Charles W. (Lt.) A. C.—Tulsa, OK
Cable, Dwight R.—Tucson, AZ
Callison, Billy—Benton, AR
Cape, Jack—Pauls Valley, OK
Carter, Godfrey G.—Concord, NH
Castle, Lyle W.—Rock Falls, IL
Castro, Raymond—Walsenburg, CO
Catchings, Virgil L.—Taft, TX
Caudle, Robert L.—Poplar Bluff, MO
Chandler, W. E. (Major) 26th Cav.
Conrad, Daniel O.—Spencer, IN
Coon, Phillip W.—Okeniah, OK
Cotten, John—Bartlesville, OK
Coyle, James R.—Helena, MT
Crane, Stanley H.—Seattle, WA
Dacenzo, Edward H.—Philadelphia, PA
Dansby, Donald M.—Carlsbad, NM
de Brey, J.—Batavia, Java, Dutch East Indies
De Keyzer, I. J.—Java, Dutch East Indies
Dorman, Walter W. (Capt.)—Maryville, MO
Drake, Aaron "Ganzo"—Carlsbad, NM
Drucy, M. S.—Bellflower, CA
Dunmeir, W. J. (Major) 45th Inf.
Dupuis, Charles Francis—Manhattan, MT
East, Franklin L.[1]
Elton, Bill—Dividend, UT
Emeis W. (MULO[2] teacher)—Batavia, Java, Dutch East Indies[3]
Evans, William R.—Milwaukee, WI
Fleeger, H. J. (Major) 26th Cav.
Flores, Ruben—Las Cruces, NM
Ford, Jacob L.—San Bruno, CA
Foster, Lawson T.—Lynchburg, VA

Francisco, George—Grahman, TX

Gardener, H. R. "Hutch"—Rogers, NM

Geuskens, Francois—Bandoeng, Java, Dutch East Indies[4]

Glasscock, Claud—Los Angeles CA

Gregory, Hubert W.—Rotan, TX

Grinner, Grant—Lone Grove, OK

Gross, G. B. (Major) 45th Inf.

Haberman, Edward A.—Long Beach, CA

Ingram, Robert Walter—Lower Stonden near Shefford,
    Bedfordshire, England

Johns, Robert Lee—Albuquerque, NM

Johnson, Chester L.C. (Major) FH—Pendleton, OR

Kanally, B. B.—Albuquerque, NM

Karns, Charles F.—New Kensington, PA

Kinler, William—Staples, MN

Kirelen, Charles A.—Brownwood, TX

Knevett, Harold Maynard—London, England

Koury, George I.—Houston, TX

Kuhlman, Quentin Marion—Biggs, CA

Laird, Harley H.—Coalgate, OK

Leib, Charles W.—Pocohontas, IA

Lewis, Homer E.—Hollywood, CA

Lilly, Bryce Lewis—Tacoma, WA

Logan, Byron—University City, MO

Long, Robert L.—Hot Springs, AR

Martin, Cecil Ray—Peshaston, WA

McClilland, Jim B.—Lenox, GA

McKinley, Ellis L.—Osakis, MN

McLouth, Estie M.—Canton, IL

Menini, Carlo H.—Gallup, NM

Miller, Jesse L.—Hollydale, CA

Moffat, James R.—Inglewood, CA

Moore, Joseph W.—Squire, WV

Morrison, Lester A.—Carlsbad, NM

Nehl, Mark E.—Morristown, SD

Newton, A. J. (Lt.)—Leighj-on-Sea, Essex, England

Norquist, Ernest—Saint Paul, MN

Nuttall, J. Arlo—Ephraim, UT

O'Hara, Larry D.—Newark, OH
Opes, Fred—Wilmington, DE
Packard, Harry B. (Major)—Kennebank, ME
Patterson, William H.—Sinton, TX
Perkins, G. H.—Ennis, TX
Plodzien, Edward F.—Chicago, IL
Poole, Harold W.—Salt Lake City, UT
Powell, George R.—Hunnewell, MO
Pribbernow, Robert M.—Oshkosh, WI
Quinn, Warren S.—Savannah, GA
Rada, E. J. (retires Nov. '44; 25 yrs)
Rice, K. V.—Lansing, MI
Rodriguez, Juan J.—Luline, TX
Rollie, Edward—Gallup, NM
Rose, Frank (M/Sgt-Reg't Supply)—Winthrop, MA
Rowland, Albert—Alamo Gordo, NM
Salm, A. E.—Oakland, CA
Sandoval, Bertram—Chacon, NM
Schenk, Harold E.—Oregon, MO
Schwausch, Hermann K.—Jarrell, TX
Senkyuek, Dick—Markham, TX
Shuping, Ralph E.—Lancaster, OH
Sly, Allen N.—San Rafael, CA
Smith, Earl W. (Medic)—Monte Vista, CO
Smith, J. J.—Java, Dutch East Indies[5]
Snedden, Murray (Lt.)—Glendale, CA
Stenger, Arlo J.—San Luis, Manila, Philipines
Stewart, Wm. N.—Pittsburgh, PA
Stonolia, C.—Hobbs, NM
Tate, Frank P.—Uniontown, AL
Taylor, J. G., Jr.—Kinston, NC
Taylor, Richard—Columbus, OH
Tenney, E. Clifford—Merrill, ME
Terry, Joseph E. (Capt.)—Salt Lake City, UT
Tuggle, G. O.—Union Point, GA
Vesper, Ralph D.—Durango, CO
Villa, Raymond—Yorktown, TX
Warner, Glenn—Demming, NM

Weipert, P. Johannes—Kosaka-machi, Japan Catholic Mission
Weist—Northville, MI
Wilkes Joseph E.—Mesa, AZ

ENDNOTES

1. Earlier in Clarence's notebook, Franklin East's hometown is stated to be Pomerene, Arizona.

2. The MULO program was first created in the Netherlands in 1857 to instruct 6- to 12-year-olds in a variety of subjects. (Noordegraaf and Vonk, Editors, *Five Hundred Years of Foreign Language Teaching in the Netherlands 1450–1950* [Amsterdam: Stichting Neerlandistiek VU, 1993], 50.) By the time the program was discontinued in 1968, the MULO (meer uitgebreid lager onderwijs, or "extended primary education") was a form of secondary education for children ages twelve to sixteen. (Public Information Office, Dutch Ministry of Education, Culture and Science.)

3. Today, this location is Jakarta, Java, Indonesia.

4. Today, this location is Bandung, Java Barat Province, West Java, Indonesia.

5. Today, this location is Java, Indonesia.

Appendix B

Clarence Bramley also recorded poetry written by his fellow POWs. He rarely recorded the author. Included here is a selection of the POWs' poetry from Clarence's notebook.

Motors in the West[1]

The old man with the whiskers
was pointing straight at me.
He says "your country needs you,"
so I joined right up for three.
The recruiting sergeant told me
of the life that was the best,
but not a word was said that day
about Motors in the West.

He spoke to me in dulcet tones
As to a man of means,
Travel is what you need," he said
"Why not the Philippines?"
So now I'm here—the war is on
I never would have guessed
That this small phrase could mean so much
"Flash! Motors in the West."

153

There was a time here on the "Rock"
When life was filled with cheer.
Our main concern was how to pay
Our monthly bill for beer.
But the Club is bombed, the bar is gone,
We're in the bomb proof pressed.
"Quiet! Silence!" There it goes again.
"Flash! Motors in the West."

Somewhere the sun is shining.
Somewhere there is peace and rest.
But there's peace no more on Corregidor,
There's Motors in the West.
But MacArthur's boys will carry on,
And each will do his best,
To throw a great big monkey wrench
In those Motors in the West.

That Morning

The morning of the surrender
We were trooping o'er the hill,
The sound of tramping, tired feet
Broke the unaccustomed still.

The weary eyes of the men that morn
Saw a scene not soon forgot,
Of broken guns and broken men
Whose bodies were left to rot.

I saw the body of a youngster
Just a lad, too young to die!
One blackened, stiffened arm
He raised—pointing to the sky.

Where are you pointing, soldier,
What message would you give,
What are you trying to tell us,
The ones who are left to live?

Do you point to the place called home,
That lies across the sea?
The land that meant so much to you,
Which you never again shall see?

Or do you point to where you have gone,
To the distant golden shore,
Where men can live like brothers,
Where there isn't any war?

Or are you trying to tell us,
As o'er the hills we plod,
To raise our minds from killing
And lift our thoughts to God?

We must march and leave you now,
In spite of flesh and bone.
You may be better off than we,
Our fate is still unknown.

In twenty years when a maddened world
Is ready to fight again,
We'll remember that upraised pointing arm,
We'll hear your message then.

EPITOME

'Twas the 8th of December in '41,
And I'll bet 2 peso's there isn't one
Who manned their guns without some fear
As the Japs began their bombing career.

On Clark field they held their course,
Flying from West and partly North.
That attack was with some surprise
And many a man is not now alive
Who gave his all for liberty.

Tactfully we maneuvered as we
Countered the attack,
Until we ended up in Bataan,
Our own cul-de-sac.
We had no Christmas turkey but
Instead a quick cold snack
There wasn't time for turkey,
We were busy falling back.

On New Years Day it was hot and clear
In the full prime of life over here,
And "For the Sake of Auld Lang Syne, My Dear,"
Was sung without a drop of cheer.
We sweat those bombers both night and day,
But chow time was their time to play.

Our rations were rapidly growing short,
Soon we went on quarter rations
Of rice, coffee and palay.
As we took up our positions
Round Cacaben and Lamay.
We even ate iguana and native monkey stew
Tho the men were feeling rather weak
Such chow might pull 'em thru—

Tojo's planes came daily over
Observing units in the clover,
While the bores were rusting in our AA guns,
We tried subterfuge and ruses
Waiting for mechanical fuses
Which would surely put the Nips on the run.

The Nipponese flew a path of roses
While they gaily thumbed their noses
At our gallant AA Coast Artillery Corps.
Then we burst our shells right in behind 'em
Which was grimly to remind 'em
That they'd never thumb their noses anymore.

Dawned the 9th day of April in forty-two,
And among us now are very few
Who won't remember that day and year
And the Nippon tanks and bombardier.

The Nips poured in planes and tanks
They rammed our fronts and walled our flanks
While we waited for the help that didn't come.
To fight on to the end was of little use
So then we flew the flag of truce,
Our defense of Bataan was nearly done.

From warriors to war prisoners
Was our sudden transformation
The fact that most of our lives were
Spared was little consolation
The condition of our mind and souls
Were stark depravity,
At failure of our help to come
From far across the sea.

From Mariveles to O'Donnell wash
Long soul searing march
Hunger, thirst and deprivation
Was our fare from dawn to dark,
And days on end we plodded
On that scorched and burning trail,
For some it was a bit too tough
Their gallant effort was to fail.

In Prison Camp O'Donnell, disease
Was quickly given birth,
Dengue fever, plus nostalgia,
Jaundice and malaria chill
Made a steady mounting population
In the place we call Boot Hill.

Unsalted rice was fancy eatin' now
Tho we got it thrice each day
Which was one mess in addition
To what we had down on the bay.
Water ration was a hardship
It was for cooking only and for a drink
But never minded we our hardships
But of greater things we'd think.

Soon the situation lightened and
Our chow it did improve.
For some salt and wormy flour
Put us right in the groove.
Now and then we had comities
Notice turnips and some greens,
But such chow increased the going
from the bahays to latrines.

Our vitamins were on the wane,
We had growing need for cuan[2]
'round the time we left O'Donnell
And moved to Cabanatuan.
Our pangs of hunger were acute
And we couldn't satisfy
The belly hunger that comes from
Living on that damned eternal palay.

At first we built small ovens out
Of nothing that was new
We thought we'd like some bread

For in our mixed and motley crew
Were some who hadn't tasted biscuits
Since back yonder on the Kouan
When they paused to take up fighting
To get democracy's arrangement.

Next we built some larger ovens
Out of Luzon's best veneer.
From stones and scraps
All chinked with mud by U.S. pioneers.

Just leave it to the Americans
We got some sour dough
And soon had some golden crusted buns
"Bout thirty dozen rows.
Twice we had some cinnamon rolls
And once some small hot cakes,
Which only whet our appetites for
Some cooking in the States.

We didn't get the flour often
And in fact it was a treat
Just to get a prison bun
Was some outstanding feat
Of doing details or performing
In our prison camp shows
Which happened twice in every fortnight
Unless postponed by tropic blows.

The eatin' nest was pretty slim
On just rice and water brew
The men were dying by the hundreds
Cause they couldn't pull it through
On such fare as burnt rice coffee
Rationed 'bout once a month
And just lugao every A.M.
Without even toast to dunk.

We even started up some classes
Of languages and such
Yea! We had some mighty scholars
Who were qualified as such
As any prof. upon the campus
Of a university
We had Economics classes,
Civics and U.S. History.

The economics problem clouded as
We tightened up our belt.
The pangs of hunger were most keen
When need for cuan most keenly felt.
The cuan came in varied items but
Mostly fish canned in Japan
With now and then a boiled egg
To slice upon an opened can.
We got some coconuts too, and
Once a can of Pork and Beans.
The sausage most was rancid fat
And with very little lean.

If we could live on rumors
We'd be rolling deep in fat
When the troops from home come
Steaming in to see where we are at
The rumors came in by the dozen
Morning, night and noon.
Their magnitude approached
Proportions of a P.I. typhoon.

How much to pay was the big question
Our cash was getting mighty low.
We hadn't had a cent of pay
Since the devastating blow.
Ten pesos for a can of beans and
Corned Willy twenty p's.

You see the cuan was hard to get
So they put us in the squeeze.
Contented cow sold two for ten
Big cans of fish were twenty
And hard boiled eggs a peso each.
By jove! There wasn't plenty.

Sometimes Vienna sausage and
Some chili peppers green
Was all the cuan that one could buy
From some leather necked Marine.
Then the commissary started and
This increased our cuan in stock
And cut in half the profit earning
By the men from on the Rock.

We turned to that philosophy
With now and then a gripe or bitch
But most cheerful just in serving
Out our prison hitch.
Our thoughts were most of the future
When we would say, "Remember when"
We were Bataan's defender,
We sons of God and men.

A SOLDIER IN OLD BATAAN

The airplanes ceased their bombing
The field guns stood grim and still
The smoke and haze of battle
Hung low over a distant hill.
The sun was slowly sinking,
Its golden rays shot down
Upon the dead and dying
Upon the battle ground.

And one among the dying,
A youth not yet a man,
Who was drafted from dear old Georgia
To fight in old Bataan.

His brother knelt beside him
As his life blood ebbed away,
And (held) his head in pity
To hear what he might say.
The dying brother looked up
And whispered, "Brother Jack,"
Take this message to mother
If ever you get back.
Jack's tears began to fall faster
As he clasped his brother's hand,
And listened to the message
He must take back from Bataan.

Tell mother how I died, Jack,
On Bataan's wide battlefield,
Where bullets rained so thickly
And flashing steel met steel.
Tell her how they promised us
They would send planes and men
And tell her how we waited, Jack,
For ships that never came in.
This hope was always burning
In the heart of every man,
But at last we knew it was hopeless
For the boys in old Bataan.

Tell her how we fought, Jack,
Together side by side
And death which swept around us
Was like a sweeping tide.
Tell her how we lived, Jack,
With only rice to eat,

Some boiled coconut or banana stalks
And sometimes a little caribao meat.
Tell her not to weep for me
For waiting I will stand
At the Golden Gate of heaven
The boy from old Bataan

And there's another, brother Jack,
That little Dixie girl.
I'm sure that she is waiting
On the other side of the world.
She kissed me as we parted
and whispered "Goodbye, Jack,
I'll be waiting here in Georgia
Longing till you get back.
So, brother, take this trinket,
Tis but a golden band,
To my sweetheart who is waiting
For her soldier in old Bataan.

His brother saw him falter,
And laid him gently back,
And heard him softly whisper,
"I must leave you now, dear Jack."
He saw his eyelids quiver,
As they closed so very slow,
He realized that his brother
Was here on earth no more.
"Oh God, receive his lovely soul,
'tis the end of life's small span,
The brother of my childhood,
Who died in old Bataan."

That night the pale moon rose
And calmly it shone down
Upon a solemn funeral
On Bataan's battleground.

His buddies offered up a prayer
There beneath a mango tree,
And someone sang
"Nearer My God to Thee."
The bamboo seemed to bow its head
There in that war torn land,
While the soldier boy was laid to rest
In a grave in old Bataan.

HEROES MODERNE

With bated breath and awestruck ear
We heard the sentence loud and clear
Ten men must die, we heard him say,
And we stood unbelieving that fateful day.

The ten men knew that they must die,
Although for truth they knew not why.
Their lives had run their brief, short span,
They were paying the debt of another man.

We saw them die that (very?) day,
Small solace they died "the American way."
Hearts for them at home will bleed
For the price they paid, there was no need.

Of heroes I've often heard and read,
But those ten men who now are dead.
We salute them one, we salute them all,
Ten finer heroes ne'er did fall.

As o'er the resting place the sod does form
A spot in our hearts for them stays warm,
For we who knew them in the past
Know full well their glory shall last.

FORGOTTEN MEN

In a camp of Nip's barracks
Lost deep in the Philippines
Lay a bunch of forgotten warriors
With nothing left but dreams.

Who are fighting a greater battle
Than the one they fought and lost.
It's a battle against the elements
A battle with life the cost.

Some came through that awful torture,
Of days and nights of hell,
In that struggle for the little "Rock,"
Where many brave men fell.

But now it's not how much you know
Or how quick you hit the ditch,
It's not the rating you once held
Or whether you're poor or rich.

No one cares who you knew back home
Or what kind of life you led,
It's just how long you can stick it out
That covers your lot instead.

The battle they're fighting at present
Is against the flies, mosquitoes and disease,
But with decent living conditions
They could win the fight with ease.

It's rice for breakfast, noon and night
And rain most every day.
We sleep on bamboo mats each night,
We've no better place to lay.

We eat from any old tin can
That we're lucky enough to get,

And the medicine we should have
We haven't seen as yet.

We're the forgotten men of yore
Fighting the hardest battle yet,
Fighting for mere existence
Thru' hunger, sickness and sweat.

And those who do come thru
Perhaps can prove their worth
When they tell the strangest story told
Of a terrible hell on earth.

PRISON IMPRESSIONS

Within the gate of a prison camp
The world seems devoid of love
But should one's glance stray upward
They'd behold God's wide world above.

The days seem endless within this camp,
One's spirits rise and fall,
But give one thought to God above,
These vanish one and all.

Should doubt of release assail your mind
Within these prison gates,
Think of God's wide world above
And the reward for those who wait.

VINDICATION[3]

"The younger generation—that is the war babies now reached maturity—seems utterly incapable of taking on the responsibilities of the nation. They are aimless, soft, and generally immature, etc." (Article read in 1939.)

They said we were soft, we were aimless
They said we were spoiled past reclaim
We had "lost the American spirit,"
We were "blots on America's name."

We were "useless, weaklings and drifters,"
And the last youth census reveals
We had "lost the faith of our Father,"
We had "sacrificed muscles for wheels."

The old men wept for their country
And sighed for the days of yore,
And somehow we half believed them
But that was before the war.

Before we had heard the bomb-shriek
And the howling, ugly and shrill,
That ripples across the rice fields,
When the "Nippy" comes in for the kill.

Before we had lived on hunger,
And rumors and nerves and pain,
Before we had seen our buddies
Dying among the cane.

Our war! Our own little rat trap!
The hopeless defense of Bataan—
An advance guard with no main body,
Yet a thorn in the flesh of Japan.

So now we can laugh at our elders
And now we can give them the lie,

We held the "line that couldn't be held,"
When they struck us at Abucay.

Soft? And weaklings? And shameless?
Go where the steel was sewed!
Ask of the endless fox graves
That dot the Harienda Road.

And ask of the tangled thickets,
Deadly and green and hot,
And the bloody Pilar River,
And the forward slopes of Sumat.

Ask at Limay and Bilanga
Where the outpost burrowed like moles,
Where the sky-trained flying soldiers
Died in their infantry holes.

And last, seek the silent jungles
Where the unburied remnants lie,
Asleep by their rusting rifles,
The men who learned how to die.

Who squeezed the Garand's trigger?
Who met the tanks on a mare?
Who flew the primary trainers
When "zeros" were in the air?

Who watched the bomb bays open
Day after endless day?
Stayed with their anti-aircraft
With tons of H.E.'s on the way?

Who led the Scouts at Quinan?
Who stopped the break at Maron?
Who but your "immature youngsters,"
The desperate men of Bataan.

So now we have learned our lesson
And how to apply it too,
And this is the application,
The things that they said were true?

We were soft, we were weaklings and aimless,
We believed in ourselves alone,
But now we are tempered with fire,
We are ready U.S. to come home.

BENEATH THE LIGHTS OF HOME

I can see these lights of home
Shining brightly o'er the foam,
Beckoning to me while I roam
Away from the lights of home.

I can see somebody there,
Laughing eyes and silver hair,
I can see her kneel in prayer,
Beneath the lights of home.

In that little old sleepy town
Nothing happens when the sun goes down
Not a thing but moonbeams roam around
Beneath the starry dome.

Turn the hands of time for me
Let me live in my memory.
Once again I long to be
Beneath the lights of home.

BATAAN

The jungles of Bataan are quiet now,
No longer torn by bomb and shell,
White crosses in the jungle gloom
Show where tortured bodies fell.

Exotic orchids grace the jungle's tallest trees,
Birds of gorgeous plumage fill the air with song,
Yet white crosses mutely speak
"Dear God," ours was not the wrong.

We fell, the dust was red like wine
With blood from tortured flesh and bone.
We died, to dust returned our mortal clay,
Our soul winged upward home.

"The Spirit" no bomb or shell can conquer
Lies not where bodies fell,
Leads on, our comrades bravely follow
Where men are beasts and earth is hell.

PRISONER'S PRAYER

Oh Lord of all who reigns on high,
I see thy works up in the sky,
The brilliant gold of every dawn,
The sunsets, beauties finely drawn,
And see at times thy pure rainbow,
A promise true to us below.

I lift my eyes up to the hills
And like the psalmist my heart fills
With strength to carry on the fight,
To live for freedom and the right.
My thanks, O' Lord for all you made,
And thy rich grace that gives me aid.

For what we have we give our thanks,
Those riches never found in banks,
For shelter, clothing and our food,
No matter if it may be crude,
But most I thank Thee for the peace
That brings to our frail hearts surcease.

How long, Lord God, of all that's just,
Must we as prisoners here rust.
We are beneath the enemy
But give us strength and power to see
Beyond this military jail
When we're delivered from travail.

And through the years on out ahead
My gratitude will ne'er go dead,
But rather I will keep in mind
The blessings of most every kind.
Recall Thy mercy in these days,
And sing to Thee eternal praise.

Unsung Heroes[4]

As I lay here in the twilight
And the day is nearly done,
I cannot help but ponder
As I watch the setting sun,
And the pals now gone forever
Who were taken in their prime
Not by bullets or by bombings
But by age, old Father Time.

Though I blame their fatal passing
On the wily Japanese,
It is entered for the records

As a tropical disease.
Beri-beri was the comment
While they buried several score,
Dysentery and malaria
Both had claimed their share and more.

We were dying by the thousands
With no relief in sight.
It was then the U.S. Army
Faced its very toughest fight.
Yes, the heroes were in plenty
On the mountains of Bataan,
But the ones we're now producing
Make them look like "also ran."

Day by day they face the struggle,
It continues through the night,
And their battle cry, like Butler's,
Is "We've just begun to fight."
Just to whom am I referring
As the heroes of this game?
Who are all those brave contenders
For the halls of mortal fame?

There's no array of medals
To decorate the breast
Just an arm band with a red cross
But it sure has stood the test.
For the most the war was over
When each man gave up his gun,
But for them the war was starting
With a fight from sun to sun.

Yes the heroes who have battled,
Never ceasing in their fight,
From the early rays of morning
To the dawn of early light,

Are the "medics" never ceasing
As they face each new born day,
Fight to save another soldier
Who has fallen by the way.

Their's is far, far graver danger
Than the battle of war,
For they daily face the danger
Of diseases' fatal scar.
They are heroes, don't forget it,
Though not mentioned by the pen,
And their fight continues daily,
Just to save the lives of men.

No medals theirs, with papers
Giving credence to the story
How they slew a hundred men,
For war's eternal glory.
No, the payment they are given
As they face each setting sun,
Is the knowledge that they face it
With a job that's been well done!

BATAAN BLUES

Oh, we are near Mariveles mountain
In the province of Bataan,
We stopped old Tojo in his tracks,
We're better man for man.
The papers say "Help is on the way,"
But gosh, where is that man?
We've looked for Yanks for many weeks
With salmon in our pans.

P-40's daily take the air
And play near Subic Bay,
Old Tojo in a wild report
Said fifty-four were there.
Now, if a few P-40s
can multiply in flight,
Maybe a convoy of one boat
Would start an awful fight.

Now if we want back Luzon
For a base against Japan
Just clean up Java some dark night
And we'll fix a place to land.
Just shake the lead out over there,
We'll use it over here,
We've lived on rice and fish too long,
Please, convoy, bring us beer.

The birds will sing of MacArthur's men
And the Battle of Bataan,
We fought the Japs from north to south,
We withdrew but never ran.
We've hunted Japs both day and night,
In holes and up in trees,
But the devils are as elusive
As a balmy summer breeze.

We had a lot of messages
By pamphlets from the air
But before we ever had them read
The bombers too were there.
They offered "co-prosperity,"
In the Asiatic sphere.
They said, "This war is not for you,
We love you, brother dear."

They sank our barge of cigarettes,
They said "So sorry, Joe,
But if you don't give up real quick
It's in the drink you go."
The Thirty-first said "Great big words,
You've never hurt us yet,
We'll have your hide in Tokyo.
On that you sure can bet."

Oh! There are DSCs and SSGs
And glory for the taking,
But give me a ticket on a great big boat
And I'll stop my belly aching.

MUD

Have you ever been in a place
That always seems to be muddy—
Especially when you must chase
Like mad to a dark brown study?

I've made mud pies as a little kid,
And I've seen the mud in the old brick yard.
I used to like it, as most of us did,
But to leave it now would not be hard.

We don't have many places to go,
But we do have to get to the "head,"
Altho' as you must also know,
At night there's a quan can instead.

In spite of our engineers,
And all of the ditches and stuff,
Long after the rain disappears,
The going is still very rough.

You wonder as you slide around,
And grope through the blackness of nite,
How you'll keep your stern end off the ground
If your timing is not quite right.

It's bad enough during daylight hours,
When you can see and not just feel,
But at night it taxes a victim's powers,
And his feelings are hard to conceal.

So when a sunshiny day comes 'round,
As they do, every now and then,
Considerable happiness can be found,
Even though you are in a "pen."

At the risk of preaching a bit,
As a Chaplain must always do,
I'm sure there's no doubt of it
That mud has a lesson for you.

No matter how much mud there may be,
Bright sunshine will always replace,
The sloppiest stuff you ever will see
And bring a smile to your face.

Let's have the sunshine as soon as you please,
For though we can take the mud for awhile,
I assure you we'll feel more at ease
When we bask in the light of a smile.

ENDNOTES

1. "Motors" refers to the Japanese aircraft that attacked the Philippines. Most of the attacking planes approached from the west.

2. Cuan (also quan or kwan) loosely described food scavenged from any available source. A quan can was used to hold or carry any item, especially food.

3. H. G. L., Cabanatuan Concentration Camp, December 1942, P.I.

4. Samuel E. Paolo, S/Sgt.

Appendix C

INTERNET URL REFERENCES

Chapter 3, endnote 1. Gordon Chappell, "Hamilton Air Force Base," accessed June 21, 2014, http://www.militarymuseum.org/HamiltonAFB.html (site discontinued).

Chapter 4, endnote 2. "Curtiss P-40E Warhawk," *National Museum of the US Air Force*, accessed December 3, 2014, http://www.nationalmuseum.af.mil/factsheets/factsheet.asp?id=478.

Chapter 5, endnote 3. Michael Gough, "Failure and Destruction, Clark Field, the Philippines, December 8, 1941," accessed Sept. 3, 2014, http://www.militaryhistoryonline.com/wwii/articles/failureanddestruction.aspx.

Chapter 6, endnote 1. Frank Steiger, "POW Diary of Captain George Steiger," copyright 1997, accessed Sept. 2, 2014, http://www.fsteiger.com/gsteipow.html. Clarence later recorded MacArthur's statement in his notebook.

Chapter 6, endnote 2. PT (Patrol-Torpedo) boats were fast attack boats used by the US Navy to attack larger surface ships. ("PT boat," *Wikipedia*, last modified December 9, 2014, http://en.wikipedia.org/wiki/PT_boat.)

Chapter 6, endnote 3. Jennifer L. Bailey, *Philippine Islands: the U.S. Army Campaigns of World War II*, essay for US Army Center of Military History, with introduction by M. P. W. Stone, Secretary of the Army, p. 19, accessed September 2, 2014, http://www.history.army.mil/html/books/072/72-3/CMH_Pub_72-3.pdf.

Chapter 6, endnote 4. Frank Hewlett, United Press International, "The Battling Bastards of Bataan," accessed Sept. 2, 2014, http://www.proviso.k12.il.us/bataan%20web/BBBPoem.html.

Chapter 6, endnote 5. Jay-Raymond N. Abad, "A King Among Men: The Story of a Forgotten General," August 2008, accessed Sept. 2, 2014, http://thephideltlegacy.com/articles/king/forgotten_general.

Chapter 6, endnote 7. This quote appears in Clarence's notebook and was recorded sometime after his capture. It has been subsequently published in various forms. (cf. The Defenders of Bataan and Corregidor [http://defendersofbataanandcorregidor.org (site discontinued)], New Mexico State University [http://reta.nmsu.edu/bataan/curriculum/resources/oral%20histories/banegas01.html], and LIFE Magazine [George Johnston, "MacArthur—A Great American Soldier Does A Great Job in Southwest Pacific," July 5, 1943].)

Chapter 6, endnote 8. Bureau of Naval Personnel Information Bulletin (March 1944). March 2002 Newsletter, *The Bataan Banner*, accessed December 17, 2014, http://www.battlingbastardsbataan.com/deathmarch.htm.

Chapter 7, endnote 1. Jennifer L. Bailey, *Philippine Islands: the U.S. Army Campaigns of World War II*, "Philippine Islands: 7 December 1941–10 May 1942," essay for US Army Center of Military History, with introduction by M. P. W. Stone, Secretary of the Army, p. 19–20, accessed September 4, 2014, http://www.history.army.mil/html/books/072/72-3/CMH_Pub_72-3.pdf.

Chapter 9, endnote 4. Linda Goetz Holmes, *Unjust Enrichment: How Japan's Companies Built Postwar Fortunes Using American POWs* (Mechanicsburg, Pennsylvania: Stackpole Books, 2001). Journal of the Taiwan POW Camp HQ in Taihoku, Exhibit "O" in Doc. No. 2687, accessed December 17, 2014, http://www.warbirdforum.com/murder.htm.

Chapter 10, endnote 1. Chad N. Proudfoot, "Hellships of World War II," *West Virginia Division of Culture and History*, copyright 2014, accessed December 17, 2014, http://www.wvculture.org/history/wvmemory/vets/hellships.html.

Chapter 10, endnote 2. On one such ship, the *Junyo Maru* (順陽丸), of 5,620 POWs aboard, approximately 4,720 died when the ship was sunk. See "Japanese Hell Ships—POW Deaths," *Militarian*, accessed December 17, 2014, http://www.militarian.com/threads/japanese-hell-ships-pow-deaths.306/#post-5076. Updated from previous edition's link: http://ww2chat.com/forums/allied-pows/306-japanese-hell-ships-pow-deaths.html (accessed May 4, 2009).

Chapter 10, endnote 3. Major Richard M. Gordon, "Remarks at the Manila American Cemetery," Ft. Bonifacio, Makati, Manila, Philippines (April 2, 2002), accessed January 10, 2007, http://reta.nmsu.edu/bataan/curriculum/resources/articles/maj_gordon_memorail_speech.pdf.

Chapter 10, endnote 4. "The Hell Ships," *Bataan Corregidor Memorial*

Foundation of New Mexico, accessed December 10, 2014, http://www.angelfire.com/nm/bcmfofnm/hellships/hellships.html.

Chapter 10, endnote 6. "When and How to Kill American POWs, Japanese Rules on Hellships," accessed January 10, 2007, www.west-point.org/family/adbc/stories_files/regulations.htm (site discontinued). See also "Regulations for Prisoners," accessed December 9, 2014, http://www.britain-at-war.org.uk/WW2/Hell_Ships/html/regulations_for_prisoners.htm.

Chapter 10, endnote 9. Bramley's journal identifies the camp as "Inringai, Taiwan." The name "Inrin Temporary Camp" was coined by Michael Hurst MBE, Taiwan POW Camps Memorial Society, http://www.powtaiwan.org.

Chapter 12, endnote 6. "Hiroshima and Nagasaki Death Toll," *Children of the Atomic Bomb*, a research website project developed by Dr. James N. Yamazaki, UCLA professor emeritus of pediatrics, together with the UCLA Asian American Studies Center. (Last modified October 10, 2007, accessed June 24, 2014, http://www.aasc.ucla.edu/cab/200708230009.html.)

Chapter 16, endnote 3. Robert C. Daniels, "MacArthur's Failures in the Philippines, December 1941–March 1942," copyright 2007, accessed Sept. 4, 2014, http://www.militaryhistoryonline.com/wwii/articles/macarthursfailures.aspx.

Chapter 16, endnote 4. See ibid. Jennifer L. Bailey, *Philippine Islands: the U.S. Army Campaigns of World War II*, "Philippine Islands: 7 December 1941–10 May 1942," essay for US Army Center of Military History, with introduction by M. P. W. Stone, Secretary of the Army, p. 19–20, accessed September 4, 2014, http://www.history.army.mil/html/books/072/72-3/CMH_Pub_72-3.pdf. Mark Douglas, *MacArthur's Pacific Appeasement, December 8, 1941: The Missing 10 Hours*, (Bloomington, Indiana: Trafford Publishing, 2012).

Chapter 16, endnote 10. "American Experience," *PBS*, accessed March 25, 2009, http://www.pbs.org/wgbh/amex/bataan/peopleevents/e_geneva.html.

Appendix D

ARCHIVAL PHOTOS

Clarenece Bramley, age 13.
Bramley Collection.

President Franklin D. Roosevelt signs the Declaration of War against Japan, December 8, 1941. *National Archives.*

Nichols Field, Philippines, 1941. *USAF Museum Photo Archives.*

P-40B aircraft of the 20th Pursuit Squadron, Nichols Field, Luzon, Philippines, 1941. *US Air Force.*

Gen. Douglas MacArthur wades ashore during initial landings at
Leyte, P.I., October, 1944. *National Archives.*

Americans raise US flag on Mt. Suribachi, Iwo Jima, on February 23, 1945.
Photo by Joe Rosenthal. *National Archives.*

USS Bunker Hill hit by two kamikazes in 30 seconds on May 11, 1945, off Kyushu, leaving 372 dead and 264 wounded. *National Archives.*

Returning from Japan, Enola Gay lands at Tinian, August 6, 1945. *National Archives.*

US postage stamp issued in July, 1945, commemorating Iwo Jima victory. *National Archives.*

US Army Air Corps recruiting poster, 1941. *USGOV-PD*

President Harry S. Truman at the White House announces Japan's surrender, 1945. *National Archives.*

Crowd celebrates VJ (Victory over Japan) Day in New York City, 1945.
National Archives.

Celebrating VJ (Victory over Japan) Day in Times Square, New York City, August 14, 1945. *National Archives.*

Prisoner of War (POW) Medal, awarded to
Clarence Bramley.

Bramley family, left to right, rear: Norma Jean, James Leonard, Clarence. Front: Mona, Terrea, 1957. *Bramley Collection.*

Clarence Bramley, in his 30th year as a firefighter with the Los Angeles City Fire Dept., 1979. *Bramley Collection.*

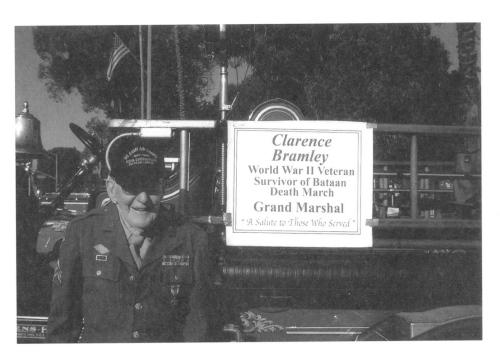

Clarence Bramley, grand marshal of Long Beach, California Veteran's Day Parade, 2010. *Bramley Collection.*

About the Author

From his own military, investigative, and legal experience, William T. Garner is able to personalize this account of the wartime service of an American soldier who became a prisoner of the Japanese. Garner, a student athlete in high school and college, is the son of a career US Marine and was himself a Marine Corps jet fighter pilot during the Korean War. Upon leaving active duty, he worked as an insurance investigator while completing the schooling he had begun before his military service. After graduation from law school and admission to the State Bar of California, he maintained a distinguished law practice in Long Beach, first alone and later as a partner in a highly respected firm. He was appointed by the governor of California to be a Judge of the Superior Court of the County of Los Angeles for the State of California and was twice elected by the people to continue in office. On the bench, from which he recently retired, he presided over many high profile criminal and civil trials. His legal career spanned nearly forty-five years, and during that time, he authored many legal decisions and treatises. In 1998, he was named "Judge of the Year" by the Long Beach Bar Association. For more than twenty years, he was also an adjunct professor of law at a local law school. In addition to his law degree, he holds a master's degree in humanities.

Garner and his wife of more than fifty-eight years, Rochelle, continue to reside in Long Beach and try to visit their six children and their families who live in several states as often as possible. During all of his adult life he has served his profession, community, and church in various capacities, and since 1991 he has been the stake patriarch in his church. He continues to teach and direct his church choir. He says of this book and of Clarence Bramley, the book's subject, "It's difficult to imagine that there is anyone who will not be touched and inspired by reading this factual account of a real American hero."